J

W9-AYO-148

Ken

HEROES OF RACING

MATT KENSETH

Speeding to Victory

by J Chris Roselius

Enslow Publishers, Inc.
40 Industrial Road
Box 398
Berkeley Heights, NJ 07922
USA
http://www.enslow.com

EAU CLAIRE DISTRICT LIBRARY

Library of Congress Cataloging-in-Publication Data
Roselius, J Chris.
   Matt Kenseth : speeding to victory / J Chris Roselius.
      p. cm. — (Heroes of racing)
   Summary: "A biography of NASCAR sports star Matt Kenseth"—Provided by publisher.
   Includes bibliographical references and index.
   ISBN-13: 978-0-7660-3000-8
   ISBN-10: 0-7660-3000-8
   1. Kenseth, Matt.—Juvenile literature. 2. Automobile racing drivers—United States—Biography—Juvenile literature. I. Title.
   GV1032.K455R67 2008
   796.72092—dc22
   [B]
                                        2007016076

Credits
Editorial Direction: Red Line Editorial (Bob Temple)
Editor: Sue Green
Designer: Becky Daum

Printed in the United States of America

10 9 8 7 6 5 4 3 2 1

To Our Readers: We have done our best to make sure all Internet addresses in this book were active and appropriate when we went to press. However, the author and the publisher have no control over and assume no liability for the material available on those Internet sites or on other Web sites they may link to. Any comments or suggestions can be sent by e-mail to comments@enslow.com or to the address on the back cover.

Disclaimer: This publication is not affiliated with, endorsed by, or sponsored by NASCAR. NASCAR®, WINSTON CUP®, NEXTEL CUP, BUSCH SERIES and CRAFTSMAN TRUCK SERIES are trademarks owned or controlled by the National Association for Stock Car Auto Racing, Inc., and are registered where indicated.

Photo credits: Jim Cole/AP Images, 1; Mary Altaffer/AP Images, 4; Mike Roemer/AP Images, 7; Rusty Burroughs/AP Images, 9; Joe Cavaretta/AP Images, 10; Chuck Luzier/AP Images, 20; The Capital Times, Henry A. Koshollek/AP Images, 23; Lisa Billings/AP Images, 30; Jennifer Graylock/AP Images, 36; Steve Helber/AP Images, 39, 60; Tom Strickland/AP Images, 44; Chuck Burton/AP Images, 57, 71, 111; Erik Perel/AP Images, 68, 73; Jason Babyak/AP Images, 78-79; J. Pat Carter/AP Images, 83, 104; Bob Jordan/AP Images, 84; Pablo Martinez Monsivais/AP Images, 87; Michael Kim/AP Images, 90; Tony Gutierrez/AP Images, 95; Pat Crowe II/AP Images, 100

Cover Photo: Jim Cole/AP Images

CONTENTS

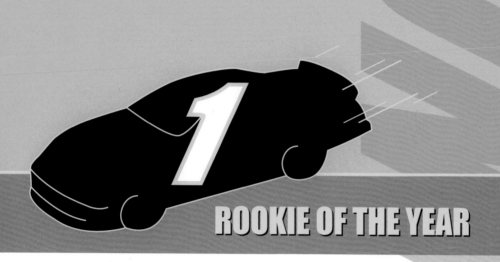

ROOKIE OF THE YEAR

Outside the state of Wisconsin, Matt Kenseth did not have a lot of name recognition. But by the end of the 2000 Winston Cup season—Kenseth's first on NASCAR's highest level—he had become a household name by winning the Raybestos Rookie of the Year award.

Kenseth was one of a host of rookies racing on the big stage in 2000. Among the crop of newcomers were Dave Blaney, Mike Bliss, Stacy Compton, and Scott Pruett. There was also one slightly more famous rookie in

Matt Kenseth smiles during an appearance at New York's Times Square on December 4, 2003.

the field—Dale Earnhardt, Jr. The son of the late Dale Earnhardt, Little E, as Earnhardt, Jr. is often called, was the rookie most people were watching—and for good reason. Not only did he learn from his father, one of the all-time great drivers, he entered his rookie campaign as the two-time defending Busch Series champion.

DID YOU KNOW?

Growing up in Wisconsin, Matt Kenseth became a huge Green Bay Packers fan. Whenever he has a chance, he loves to watch the Packers on TV. Quarterback Brett Favre is one of his favorite athletes.

Kenseth, driving for Roush Racing in the DeWalt No. 17 car, established himself as a rookie to watch, too. In six of the season's first ten races, he was the top finishing rookie and was the leader in the Rookie of the Year points battle. He even had his best finish of the season up to that point when he placed third in the NAPA Auto Parts 500 at the California Motor Speedway on April 30.

Kenseth dominated for much of the race, leading for 120 laps. But he came up short in the end, thanks mostly to a yellow caution flag. Coming into pit lane as the leader, he took on four new tires and exited in fifth place. Despite his front-running status throughout the race, Kenseth had a bad feeling much of the day.

Green Bay Packers quarterback Brett Favre signs a jersey for Matt Kenseth before a game in 2003.

"I just planned on losing all day long," he said. "I knew something was going to happen, and the minute I was thinking to myself, 'Boy, we are in pretty good shape,' sure enough, something happened."[1]

BREAKING THROUGH

Kenseth's bad luck did not last long. On deck was the longest race of the year, the Coca-Cola 600 at Lowe's Motor Speedway. Earnhardt, Jr., in the midst of a successful run, claimed the pole for the big race.

Kenseth, meanwhile, was stuck in the middle of the pack with a starting position of twenty-first. But he did not stay there long.

From the start, the DeWalt No. 17 car was strong. Staying with the leaders lap after lap, Kenseth deftly advanced toward the front of the field before rain delayed the race on Lap 258 for nearly an hour.

The delay proved beneficial to Kenseth. With the green flag waving, signaling the start of racing action, Kenseth shot into eighth place and quickly gained on the rest of the field. The key point in the race came during the final pit stop. The pit crew got Kenseth in and out of pit lane in 16.5 seconds, allowing him to come back onto the track in second place, trailing only Bobby Labonte.

On Lap 275, Kenseth seized the lead. He opened up an unbeatable margin with ten laps remaining and went on to claim his first Winston Cup victory in his eighteenth career start. After becoming the first rookie to win NASCAR's longest race, he did several donuts in the infield grass and then drove backward for his victory lap.

"It hasn't sunk in too much," Kenseth said after the race. "I really don't even know how to act. I didn't think we were going to run as good as we did tonight. I thought we would maybe be in the top 10 and have a good competitive run, but I certainly wasn't expecting to win the race.

Kenseth's crew members celebrate their win in the 2000 Coca-Cola 600.

"It's a relief to get the first win. With Tony (Stewart) winning three races last year, and Junior already winning two this year, there's a certain pressure I put on myself that we need to take that step and win a race. We've done everything we could all year to try to do that. It's not that we did something different or something magic this weekend, it's just how it worked out for us."[2]

A WIN WAS ALL HE NEEDED

The Coca-Cola 600 victory lifted Kenseth to thirteenth in the points standings and vaulted him into first place in the Rookie of the Year race with 154 points, compared to 149 for Earnhardt, Jr. Kenseth never looked back.

Kenseth spins in the infield after a win in Las Vegas.

He placed second the following week at Dover in the MBNA Platinum 400 and claimed six more top-ten finishes, including a fifth-place showing at Pocono in the Pennsylvania 500.

Kenseth finished seventeen of the thirty-four races as the highest-placing rookie and ended up with a total of four top-five finishes and eleven top-ten finishes, which topped all rookies. His average finishing position of nineteenth also led all rookies. Kenseth's consistency allowed him to finish atop the Rookie of the Year points standings with 316 points. Earnhardt, Jr., the preseason favorite, placed second with 274 points. Kenseth finished fourteenth overall in the Winston Cup standings.

Kenseth wrapped up the rookie points title with a ninth-place finish at the NAPA 500 in Atlanta after qualifying twenty-third. Afterward, Kenseth was happy to be the top rookie while also praising his main competition for the award.

"It's a real honor to accept this award," Kenseth said. "To come out on top of this great group of rookies is really special. Dale Jr. is a great racecar driver who beat us in Busch the last two years, and I knew he'd be tough again this year. He had some bad luck during the middle part of the season that helped us get ahead.

"You're going to see him win many more races and championships in the future. Dave Blaney came on strong at the end of the year, and the rest of the guys, Stacy Compton, Mike Bliss, and Scott Pruett, all have bright careers ahead of them. To finish ahead of that caliber of talent says a lot about the commitment and talent of this race team."[3]

MATT KENSETH FILE

Height: 5' 9"

Weight: 150 lb.

Date of Birth: March 10, 1972

Hometown: Cambridge, Wisconsin

Team: Roush Racing

Crew Chief: Robbie Reiser

PROVING HIMSELF AT DAYTONA

NASCAR fans should not have been surprised with Kenseth's outstanding season. He showed in the season-opening race, the Daytona 500—the Super Bowl of NASCAR—that he was someone to watch.

Starting twenty-fourth in the forty-three car field, Kenseth expertly guided the No. 17 car through the congestion, climbing to seventeenth in the standings before making a pit stop. Having to again navigate through the bottleneck of cars, Kenseth languished in the middle of the pack through the next two pit stops before making a move after his last pit.

Showing skills not often seen in a rookie, Kenseth slipped past one driver and then another, allowing him to zoom into twelfth. A wreck threatened his position on Lap 192, but Kenseth avoided the pileup and maneuvered his way to a tenth-place finish.

"What a great day for the DeWalt team," Kenseth said after the race. "The car never seemed to be perfect during the race. We were tighter than we wanted to be. But this team kept after it, and we had some luck avoiding the wrecks.

"It's nice to get a good finish in our first race during our rookie season for (crew chief) Robbie Reiser and the rest of the guys. We are real happy with a top 10. They worked hard this off-season, it showed here at Daytona, and we're off to a good start."[4]

OVERCOMING A ROCKY START

The showing at Daytona boosted the spirits of Kenseth and everyone on his team, but it would be the start of a series of highlights and lowlights for Kenseth until he hit his stride at the Coca-Cola 600.

Excited about his finish at Daytona, a confident Kenseth headed to Rockingham for the Dura Lube/Kmart 400. Kenseth had a great qualifying run, placing sixth. Unfortunately, that would be the lone bright spot that weekend.

Kenseth was running in seventh place when the caution flag went up on Lap 18. Kenseth and his crew decided to keep their car on the track with the rest of the leaders instead of coming in for a pit stop.

The decision proved disastrous. Kenseth struggled with the handling of the car, and it only got worse as his tires became more worn. Pushing his car in an effort to keep up with drivers using fresher tires, Kenseth brushed the wall on the fifty-third lap.

He was forced to make a series of stops to repair the damage to the side of the car, which led to a thirty-seventh-place finish.

It looked as if Kenseth's bad luck was carrying over the next weekend in Las Vegas. While he finished fifth in the Busch series race on Saturday, Kenseth started in twenty-first position for the Carsdirect.com 400 on Sunday.

With his car performing well, Kenseth started quickly and soon found himself in seventeenth only nineteen laps into the race. Soon, he was running in second place, only to see the red flag come out due to rain. When racing resumed, Kenseth dropped to fourteenth, where he remained until the race was stopped on Lap 145 due to more rain.

While unhappy the race was not able to be completed, Kenseth was pleased with his performance, especially after the difficulties he had one week earlier.

"I felt like we could run in the top ten for sure, if we could have made one or two more adjustments," said Kenseth. "I'm never real pumped up about a 14th, but on the other hand, after last weekend and the way that went, I'm happy. A finish in the top fifteen here gains us a few points. Now we can go to Atlanta and race again."[5]

And race he did. Kenseth qualified fourth for the Cracker Barrel Old Country Store 500. He knew he had a fast car when the green flag dropped at the start of the race. Shooting up toward the front of the field, he rocketed into first place on the fifth lap, giving the rookie the lead for the first time that season.

The lead, however, did not last long. Experiencing low water pressure midway through the race, the car started to run hot. The DeWalt team did its best to keep the car cool by bringing Kenseth in for several pit stops, but nothing worked. Finally, on the 203rd lap, Kenseth was forced to leave the race when his motor blew, sending a plume of smoke out the back of his car.

Kenseth bounced back to finish sixth in the Mall.com 400 at Darlington. It was his second top-ten finish of the season and a great way to rebound after the troubles in Atlanta.

DID YOU KNOW?

When Matt Kenseth has time to watch movies, he likes to watch comedies. *Fletch* is one of his favorite movies, and he likes *Old School* a lot as well.

"We had a good racecar today," Kenseth said. "The DeWalt guys did a great job in the pits and adjusting on the car, and they gave me a car that might have been able to get a third. We were a couple of breaks away from running right up front. But that's a great finish for us. It gets us valuable points for both the championship and the rookie race."[6]

The next four races did not go as well for Kenseth. After a solid twelfth-place finish at Bristol, Kenseth placed thirty-first, twenty-first, and eighteenth in his next three outings. The results were not spectacular, but they were solid.

The only problem, however, was the lack of wins. While Kenseth was racking up points, Earnhardt, Jr., a friend away from the track but a rival on it, was grabbing the headlines.

Seven races into his career, Earnhardt, Jr. stood in the winner's circle at the end of a race after taking the checkered flag at the Texas Motor Speedway in the DirectTV 500. Four weeks later, Earnhardt, Jr. claimed his second career victory by winning the Pontiac Excitement 400 at Richmond International Raceway. He followed that win with a victory in the NASCAR all-star race, the Winston, at Lowe's Motor Speedway. The pressure was on for Kenseth to earn his first victory.

One week after Earnhardt's Winston victory, Kenseth was in the winner's circle, and by the end of the year, he was celebrating the honor of being the top rookie in 2000.

Though born in Madison, Wisconsin, Matt Kenseth grew up with his older sister, Kelley, and his parents, Roy and Nicki, in the sleepy town of Cambridge, which had fewer than 1,000 residents in 1972.

Matt had a happy childhood in Cambridge, located about 20 miles (32 kilometers) southeast of Madison. He received lots of love from his mother and father and enjoyed the typical life of a child. He spent his days with his friends at the nearby park or on the basketball court.

DID YOU KNOW?

Whenever he has the time to go on vacation, Kenseth likes to return to his roots. He enjoys traveling to Wisconsin and spending time in a little cabin he owns there.

He spent much of his time outdoors. When Matt did stay inside the house, he often played on his Atari game system. As he got older, he earned extra money by working.

But Matt was almost always doing something.

"I was a typical small-town kid," Matt said. "My dad ran a variety of small businesses. He sold furniture, operated laundry, and ran a video rental store. As a kid, I helped unload furniture and sold tickets at the local theater."[1]

Cambridge is a community where midwestern values are stressed. Residents go out of their way to be kind and courteous to both neighbors and strangers. It is a town that loves its own and wants to make sure everyone experiences success.

"(Cambridge is) a typical small town in the Midwest, a very close community," said Bob Nodolf, a former neighbor and teacher of Kenseth at Cambridge High School. "There are a lot of good things going on, people willing to help each other out. It's a tight, close-knit community. They relish their heroes—and they make it tough on you if you're not very nice."[2]

RACING NEVER FAR AWAY

Matt's environment molded him into the person he is today. He is a person who shuns the spotlight and believes hard work will result in success. But Cambridge also fueled his love for cars. He loved to watch *The Dukes of Hazard*, a popular television show, with his family or race cars with whomever would challenge him on his slot car racetrack.

If there was something with wheels or a motor—or both—Matt was often riding it around town. He also loved to take machines apart to see how they worked. There is no telling how many times he took apart his bicycle to see how all the different parts fit together and operated, only to put it back together again.

One of Matt's favorite pastimes as a kid was driving his grandfather's riding lawnmower down the streets of Cambridge. When not riding it, he was often tinkering with it to see if he could make it go faster. He also liked to go faster on his bike. A favorite picture in the Kenseth household is one of Matt sitting astride his bike, barely getting his tiptoes on the ground to keep the bike upright. In one hand Matt is holding a checkered flag with the words "Speedway Winner" on it.

DID YOU KNOW? One of Kenseth's childhood nicknames was "Motor" because Kenseth liked anything with a motor on it.

Dale Earnhardt, Kenseth's favorite driver as a youngster, waves from Victory Lane on February 9, 1986.

But Matt did not just stumble into racing. The love for speed runs through his family. Matt's uncles loved to race at Jefferson Speedway, and his father dabbled in racing as well. In the 1960s, Roy Kenseth often drag raced at Great Lakes Speedway. As Matt grew up, Saturday nights were basically reserved for watching someone in his family race.

Sunday afternoons were usually set aside for watching NASCAR racing on television with his father and grandfather. His favorite driver was Dale Earnhardt, who was known as "The Intimidator" because of his driving style.

"My dad and I never had satellite or cable," Matt said. "We'd go over to my grandfather's house and watch races. I always liked Dale Earnhardt. I thought it was cool that he drove a car so hard."[3]

While known as a southern sport, NASCAR has always been popular in Wisconsin. Through the years, the state has produced a number of top-notch drivers, such as Dave Marcis, Dick Trickle, and Alan Kulwicki, a 1992 Winston Cup champion who died in a plane crash in 1993 on his way to a race in Bristol.

"Growing up, I followed all those drivers and really admired them," Matt said. "Any time drivers from your area go on to do well, it serves as inspiration to the young guys back home. You think, 'They made it, and so can I.'"[4]

AN OFFER HE COULD NOT REFUSE

Surrounded by a family of race fans, Matt's interest in auto racing only increased as he got older. Living in a sparsely populated area allowed him an early chance to get acquainted with an automobile. Driving around on the back roads

DID YOU KNOW?

Matt Kenseth's early work fixing cars came in handy. His first car was a Honda Accord that his older sister had driven previously. Being an older car, it did not run, forcing Kenseth to work on it for about a month before it ran smoothly.

of Wisconsin with his father while he was making furniture deliveries, Matt often slid over to take the wheel of the car.

"As soon as I got where I could reach the pedals, he would let me drive," Matt said of his father. "I was probably 12 or 13. It wasn't often, just when Mom wasn't around."[5]

Matt's mother was not around when his father offered him a deal that was too good to pass up. Driving home from the racetrack one Sunday afternoon, Matt's father suggested they buy a racecar. The deal would be that Roy would drive it and Matt would work on it, learning first-hand how a car works.

Matt was wide-eyed with the possibilities of working on his own racecar and quickly agreed to the deal.

"He said, 'You'd really do that,'" said Roy Kenseth. "'Yeah, I really would.'"[6]

"My dad made me a deal when I was 13, he would buy the car and drive it if I would work on it and keep it up," Matt recalled. "Then, when I turned 16, I could drive the car. It was hard work, but it was also a great experience and really prepared me to do more than just steer the car."[7]

DID YOU KNOW?

While Kenseth admired several people growing up, his biggest childhood hero was his father, Roy. One of his favorite activities was just hanging out with his father.

Matt Kenseth and his father, Roy, stand near the new store sign showing the exterior of Matt's future MK Race Wear Store in Cambridge, Wisconsin.

Matt dove into his new duties as his father's chief auto mechanic. He loved to get his hands dirty and learn everything he could about making a racecar go faster, have better handling, or cut through the air with less resistance.

For Matt, being around racecars was his purpose in life.

"Matt's a good example of someone who is doing what he was naturally supposed to do," said his sister, Kelley Maruszewski.[8]

Today, it is hard to drive around the town of Cambridge and not be reminded that Matt Kenseth grew up there. Decals or logos depicting Matt or his

DeWalt No. 17 car are seemingly everywhere.

Matt now makes his permanent home in North Carolina, but Cambridge is still his hometown. No matter how much success he has experienced in his career, he has never forgotten where he came from. He enjoys visiting the friends he grew up with, and he has had members of his family or friends on his team's crew from the beginning of his career.

"Matt hasn't forgotten where he's come from," Nodolf, his former teacher, said. "He still comes back quite a bit when he's off. He still has a lot of good friends here and still hangs out with them. It's a real tribute to him. A lot of guys get too big, but he hasn't done that at all."[9]

DID YOU KNOW?

Kenseth enjoys a good meal. One of his favorite meals is the homemade chicken pot pie his wife, Katie, makes.

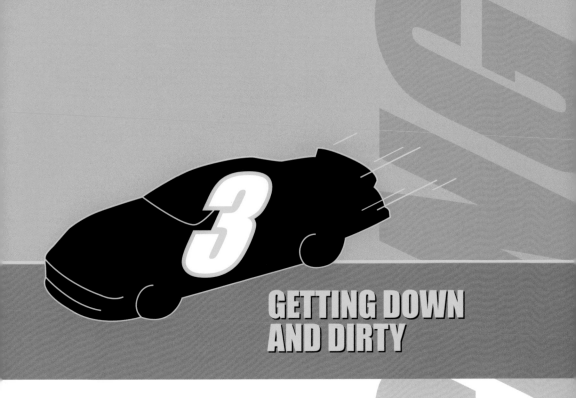

GETTING DOWN AND DIRTY

Roy Kenseth made good on his promise to his son. He purchased a 1981 Chevrolet Camaro. As soon as he was allowed, Matt was under the hood. The father-son team spent hours together as they worked on the car or raced it at the nearby tracks.

When Matt turned fifteen, his father allowed him to drive some laps at Columbus 151 Speedway. One year later, he entered his first race, driving the 1981 Camaro that he and his father had worked on for the last three years. It did not take Matt long to find

DID YOU KNOW?

In 1991, Matt Kenseth was the youngest driver to ever win an ARTGO racing series feature event. In 1994, he became the youngest driver to win the Miller Genuine Draft National Championship.

the winner's circle. One month after his first race, Matt earned his first win on July 15, 1988, at Columbus. The win changed the focus of the family. Roy had won his first feature race at Jefferson Speedway, and Matt had been there to witness the victory. But it was becoming obvious that Matt had serious talent as a racecar driver. Roy decided it was time to push his own racing career to the side to concentrate on his son's.

"My dad's always been convinced I'd succeed way more than I have, and that's true today," Matt said. "That was the third week out, and from that point out, he became second and he made me a priority. He thought it was something I could do full time, something I could have a career at."[1]

Within a year, Matt's reputation as a top-notch driver was spreading. He collected wins at Columbus, the Dells, and Plover Speedways, beating some of the top local racers along the way.

ESTABLISHING HIMSELF AS ONE TO WATCH

The victories were nice, and they fed Matt's appetite to race. But Matt wisely remained involved in the

"I got my first car when I was 16 and just started going. Since then, things actually went kind of fast. I haven't really had any time to look back at it because we're always busy trying to get better or trying to do something bigger or whatever."

— Matt Kenseth

DID YOU KNOW?

Kenseth's first race car was a 1981 Chevrolet Camaro that his father bought for $1,800. One month into his racing career, Kenseth won his first race in that car.

inner workings of the racecar. He continued to spend just as much time under the hood as he did behind the steering wheel.

Upon his graduation from high school in 1990, Kenseth went to work at Lefthander Chassis in Rockford, Illinois. He worked on engines and did some body work. Kenseth has said he learned something every day while at his job.

Kenseth enjoyed being at Lefthander Chassis, but he liked being behind the wheel even more. He competed in as many races as he could afford to enter. Soon he moved up to the late model division and became a regular at Slinger Speedway, a one-quarter-mile (.4-km), high-banked short track located about an hour from Milwaukee. The track has been home to hundreds of drivers who have gone on to the Busch and Winston/Nextel Cup series.

When Kenseth showed up, he was a scrawny eighteen-year-old. On a track known for its high speeds, bumping, and banging, the young Kenseth did not look like he was ready for the tough racing ahead. Older and more experienced drivers, such as Robbie Reiser, told him he did not have the muscle to handle the track. How wrong they were. In the season-opening race at Slinger, Kenseth came out the victor.

"He definitely turned some heads, and he did it right away," said Reiser, a top driver at the track at the time. "His second year there he was competing for wins, when a lot of the other guys—like myself—took five or six years to start winning."[2]

BREAKING OUT

The 1991 racing season would be one to remember for Kenseth. Only nineteen years old, he established himself as one of the top drivers in the state, if not the region. Racing a full schedule at Slinger Speedway, Kenseth earned the title of Late Model Rookie of the Year.

He also put his name into the record books that year. Racing in the ARTGO series, Kenseth entered an event at LaCrosse Fairgrounds. The youngest driver competing, he showed amazing skill and talent as he weaved and darted through the congested field of drivers. When the checkered flag dropped, it was

Kenseth's car crossing the finish line first, making him the youngest driver to win an ARTGO racing series feature event.

The previous record holder was Mark Martin, the man who would eventually help shape Kenseth's career.

Success on the track continued for Kenseth. He consistently ran near the front of the field, building on his success in 1991. He continued to learn about racing as well, taking what he learned from a past race and applying it in future races.

DID YOU KNOW? When not racing, Kenseth likes to ride motorcycles and enjoys boating, golf, and computer games.

In 1993, Kenseth firmly established himself as one of the region's top drivers. He won a feature in the Wisconsin Short Track Series 200 and notched two ARTGO feature races. At Slinger Speedway, he won the Alan Kulwicki Memorial race. His success at Wisconsin International Raceway earned him Late Model Rookie of the Year honors. Overall, he won six late model features that year.

SUCCESS CONTINUES ON THE TRACK

Before the start of the 1994 season, Fred Nielson, an Illinois developer and car owner, signed Kenseth to a five-year deal. Kenseth was introduced to Nielson by

Kenseth found success at local and regional tracks before debuting at NASCAR's top levels.

Joe Shear. Shear was one of the region's top short-track racers and a person who shared his knowledge with Kenseth during his time at Lefthander Chassis and on the track.

Nielson provided Kenseth with his first real professional ride. Nielson, however, knew that Kenseth was an up-and-coming driver who had grand visions about his future.

"We made an agreement that if he had the possibility to go farther, then I would be 100 percent right behind him," said Nielsen.[3]

If Kenseth was not a household name in the Midwest, he was after the 1994 season. He captured track titles at both Madison International Speedway and Wisconsin International Raceway. In fact, he set a record with twelve feature wins at Madison. Kenseth also entered the record books once again when he won the Miller Genuine Draft National Championship at Slinger, becoming the youngest champion of the two-round series.

THANKING SLINGER

One of the main rivals Kenseth beat was Reiser, his future Busch series boss and eventual crew chief on the DeWalt team. Friends now, the two were not always friendly in the early days of Kenseth's career.

"Well, we were real enemies on the track," said Roy Kenseth. "Every week Matt and Robbie would battle it out."[4]

Racing against fierce competitors such as Reiser helped Kenseth hone his skills. But Kenseth also believes growing up and racing in Wisconsin helped him become the driver he is today.

"Racing in Wisconsin was good for me because unlike down South where most local races will start the fastest guys up front, in Wisconsin, they always invert the field," Kenseth said. "If I finished up front in a heat race or a qualifying race, I would be starting in the back in the feature.

"You had to know how to pass other drivers safely, particularly if a guy's car isn't handling or if he's slow. You very rarely had an open track to race on so you always had to be on your toes and be ready for anything. Wrecks happen often, and they happened quickly."[5]

Reiser, who won three consecutive track titles at Slinger from 1991 to 1993, remembers his days at the track fondly.

"We had a lot of fun at Slinger, and I'm pretty sure I beat Matt a whole lot more than he beat me," Reiser jokingly said. "We tore up a lot of stuff, and tempers would flare. I remember one race at Slinger that Matt was chasing down the leader and it was basically a two-car race as I was running third. Matt got underneath this guy, an old Slinger veteran, and they spun out directly in front of me.

"I got on the brakes hard and was able to miss them and I made eye contact with Matt as I slid by, and his eyes were so wide. I wound up winning the race, but that was typical Slinger. That was the kind of stuff that happened."[6]

With Slinger shaping his racing ability, Kenseth continued his assault on the track. In 1995, he won the Red, White and Blue State Championship Series, recorded four consecutive feature wins at Wisconsin International Raceway and wound up with the track title at WIR.

At this point, there was nothing left for Kenseth to prove in the Midwest. It was time to test himself in the South and in the larger circuits. It was time for him to move his career forward.

TAKE IT FROM MATT

Matt Kenseth's path to the Nextel Cup circuit was not easy. He first got into racing by working on a car his father bought. He then slowly started to get in some laps sitting behind the wheel before seriously racing.

Kenseth often raced at Slinger Speedway as well as Wisconsin International Raceway and Madison International Speedway. But he also made sure he traveled to numerous other racetracks.

When asked what it takes to become a top racecar driver, Kenseth offers the following advice.

"Start at a local track and if you want to be a driver, drive whatever you can afford," he said. "Then win as many races as you can. If you want to be on a crew, start with a team locally and learn how to work on cars, and if you are hooked up with a good driver, you have a chance to move on."

Kenseth said there is no set way to progress to the highest level of racing. However, he does have one strong suggestion.

"The main thing I was lucky enough to do a lot, and I would suggest, would be to race as many different tracks as you can," Kenseth said. "Don't get stuck racing at the same track every week. I think it's really important to get out and race as many different types of racetracks as you can."

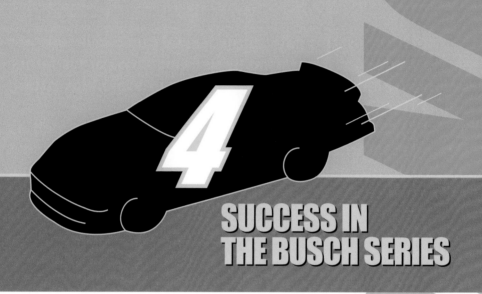

Kenseth did not have unlimited resources to help start his racing career. In fact, he was basically broke when he headed to North Carolina.

But racing on the Hooters circuit, Kenseth enjoyed some success, earning a win in South Carolina.

In May 1996, Kenseth experienced his first Busch race. Racing in a non-sponsored car rented from Bobby Dotter, Kenseth finished thirty-first in his debut at Charlotte. Kenseth hoped the showing would lead to a sponsorship deal, but one never came.

Running out of funds, Kenseth headed back to Wisconsin in 1997. Luckily, Gerry Gunderman owned a well-known American Speed Association (ASA) team, and he wanted Kenseth as his driver. The pairing of the two was a perfect match. In Kenseth's first race he finished second.

AN OPPORTUNITY HE COULD NOT PASS UP

Kenseth's second-place showing with Gunderman would be his best showing on the ASA circuit. That is because he got a call from Reiser, his old racing nemesis from Wisconsin. Now the owner of Reiser Enterprises, Reiser needed a driver to replace the injured Tony Bender for his Busch Grand National racing team.

Reiser remembered Kenseth from their racing days and offered him a six-race deal to fill in for Bender. It was the call Kenseth had been waiting for, a call that would offer him the chance to catch the eye of a NASCAR owner.

But it also put Kenseth in a tough position. A firm believer

MAKING A STRONG IMPRESSION

Kenseth was second in the ASA series points standings prior to joining Reiser Enterprises and the Busch series. Despite making only twenty-one starts, Kenseth finished second in the Rookie of the Year race.

in loyalty, he did not want to break his agreement to race for Gunderman. In the end, however, he knew he had to take Reiser's offer.

"I know I've let Gerry down, and I know I've let the guys down, but I think they understand," said Kenseth. "I talked to a lot of people before I made this decision, a lot of people I trust. I know I'm only 25, but they told me if I don't look out for Matt Kenseth, nobody else will. If after six races nothing else happens, well, then at least I got to run six races."[1]

Reiser remembered Kenseth as a competitive and talented driver.

"He could run with anybody and was as good as anybody," Reiser said. "When I started a Busch team and had to hire a driver, he was my pick because I knew he could do it."[2]

The chance proved to be life altering for Kenseth. "It's been history ever since," Kenseth said. "If I hadn't gotten that opportunity, I'd be racing somewhere in Wisconsin."[3]

PROVING HIMSELF IN A HURRY

The young driver rapidly established himself on the track. In his first race with Reiser at Nashville Speedway, he qualified third and finished eleventh. Racing at Nashville was nothing new to Kenseth. He gained experience at the track in past races there.

But his upcoming race would be a whole new experience. The schedule took Kenseth to Talladega and its Superspeedway, a track on which Kenseth would reach speeds of 190 miles per hour (306 kilometers per hour) in a Busch car that was taller and heavier than the cars he was used to driving.

Kenseth did not let the new conditions scare him. Instead, he took the opportunity during a practice

WANT TO WRITE?

Kenseth tries his best to read all of his mail, but his hectic schedule often keeps him from replying to his fans. However, for those who want to send him a letter, just mail it to Matt Kenseth at the Matt Kenseth Fan Club, 700 Kenseth Way, Cambridge, WI 53523.

run on Friday to draft behind Winston Cup veterans. It was a wise move. It helped Kenseth gain confidence in his ability to drive well on the track. And drive well was exactly what he did.

After qualifying twentieth, Kenseth moved his way up through the field and placed seventh in Saturday's race, the best finish for the Reiser team that season.

After the race, Kenseth was already talking like a seasoned veteran.

"We've been close. We've only run two races, but we haven't been too far off," Kenseth said. "If we can stay close like that and finish races, we're not going to do anything but keep getting better."[4]

Reiser saw the success Kenseth was experiencing and realized he was the driver he needed if he wanted to win on the Busch level. The original six-race deal was thrown out. Kenseth was signed to a deal through the 1998 season.

"I think it's going to work out really good," said Kenseth.[5]

The deal with Reiser did more than work out. Despite a wreck during a morning practice at the Milwaukee Mile, Kenseth was able to qualify with a backup car and finished the race in twelfth place. The crash could have easily affected his entire weekend. But Kenseth did not let the mishap slow him down. He showed everyone he was there to race.

By the end of the season, Kenseth had seven top-ten finishes and two top-five finishes, leading to a second-place showing in the Busch Rookie

Teammates Mark Martin and Matt Kenseth talk before a September 2006 race.

of the Year standings despite competing in only twenty-one races.

While he did not win any races, he did hold a lead for twenty-nine laps. A testament to his ability to race through traffic, Kenseth's average start was in twentieth place, but his average finish was sixteenth.

Kenseth got another break in 1997, perhaps one even more important than landing a ride with Reiser. During the season, he and Reiser were able to form a relationship with Roush Racing.

They were asked to travel to Darlington, where they were on hand to watch Mark Martin test on the track. It began a strong relationship between Kenseth and Martin that lasts to this day.

"Jack (Roush) wanted us to see how the whole thing worked," Reiser said. "We went there just to observe, but Mark wanted (Kenseth) to drive his car. He has never even seen Darlington. To watch him get on a track he'd never seen before and drive a car he'd never driven before and to run it just as well as Mark did, that showed me he could handle any situation that came up."[6]

The 1997 season proved to be a breakthrough year for Kenseth. Despite winning on every level in which he competed, the money he earned from those wins immediately went back into buying spare parts and fixing his racecar. Seldom was Kenseth able to save the money he earned for himself.

But thanks to his success as a Busch rookie, Kenseth earned nearly $200,000. And the connections he made with Martin and Roush Racing would prove to be vital.

After the 1997 season, Kraft Singles announced that it would not be a sponsor for Reiser Racing in 1998. Without a sponsor, racing can be an expensive endeavor. Without Kraft, the 1998 season could have been in jeopardy.

But during his weekend in Darlington testing with Martin, Kenseth was so impressive that he secured a testing contract from Roush Racing. It was a relationship that would prove to be invaluable.

BREAKING INTO THE WIN COLUMN

After finishing in the top five twice in 1997, Kenseth won three Busch races in 1998, taking the checkered flag at Rockingham, Pikes Peak, and Dover. The next year he increased his win total to four with victories at Darlington, Nazareth, Fontana, and Bristol.

MENTORS SHAPE KENSETH'S FUTURE

Throughout Kenseth's life, he has learned from different mentors. The most important mentor is his father, Roy.

Racing was always a part of the Kenseth family's life, but it was Roy who really helped spark Kenseth's desire to become a racecar driver. As Kenseth succeeded on the racetrack, his father was there every step of the way, offering encouragement or tips on how to improve. Even today, Roy is still the most important person in Kenseth's life. But he was a larger-than-life figure during Kenseth's childhood. "My biggest childhood [memory] here was my dad," Kenseth said. "I loved to do stuff with my dad and hang out with him when I was a kid."[1]

Now a NASCAR champion, Kenseth makes millions of dollars each year. But his bond with his father is as strong as ever. He often heads back home to spend time with his father during the off-season. In fact, Kenseth will go out of his way to help his father—even in the middle of the season.

In May 2003, Kenseth headed back to Madison International Speedway (MIS), a place where some of his biggest wins occurred early in his career. Kenseth was at MIS to compete in the Blain's Farm and Fleet/DeWalt 100, his first race at MIS since 1996.

Since racing at MIS, Kenseth went on to make a name for himself in the Busch series and then win the Rookie of the Year award on the Winston Cup circuit. So why was Kenseth spending one of his few off weeks at the half-mile (.8-km) oval during in the middle of the 2003 NASCAR season?

"The main reason I am going back to Madison is because of my dad. I probably would be going to the Bahamas if he wasn't working there. This is something he always wanted to do," said Kenseth.[2]

DID YOU KNOW? Kenseth said his favorite breakfast cereal is Cocoa Krispies.

Mark Martin chats with Matt Kenseth before the start of the Allstate 400 at the Brickyard.

Roy was hired by track owner Terry Kunes to promote the track. What better way to help bring in fans than by asking your now-famous son to come back for a race? And how could Kenseth say no to his father?

"Racing brought us together really, really close because we both love it," Roy Kenseth said. "He knows that by him coming up here, we're going to pack the place. It's going to help everything. Not only me, but the track and the area and everybody. Wisconsin, these are his true fans."[3]

SHEAR SHARES HIS KNOWLEDGE

Through the years, other people have had an impact on Kenseth as well. One of those people is Joe Shear.

Shear was one of the top short-track racers in the Wisconsin region for decades. He met Kenseth when he was a young, lanky kid working at the Lefthander, the stock car shop in Rockford where Kenseth was employed as a teenager.

The two struck up a friendship. Shear offered advice and answered any questions Kenseth had. But more important, Shear made sure Kenseth did not get out of line, either on the track or off it.

"If he'd see me do something stupid, he'd tell me I shouldn't be doing that stuff," Kenseth said.[4]

Shear introduced Kenseth to Fred Nielson, a meeting that helped lead to Kenseth's first professional ride. From there, Kenseth was able to make more acquaintances in the industry until meeting Martin, the veteran NASCAR driver.

A fan of NASCAR racing, Kenseth had always liked the way Martin handled himself on the track. He said Martin is one of the drivers he tries to emulate most as a driver.

"When I'm in a tough position I ask myself sometimes, 'What would Mark Martin do?' Mark is a fair driver," Kenseth said. "He's a tough driver when he needs to be, but he races smart every lap. He's not going to beat himself, and he usually keeps his equipment in good shape for the end of the race. I try to do the same, and I'd say Mark is the one I look to on the track as a great example of how to race people."[5]

A TRUE MENTOR

Martin first noticed Kenseth in 1997 and immediately saw a driver who could have success on the Winston/Nextel Cup level. It was Martin who offered Kenseth the chance to test drive one of his cars at Darlington. Martin also helped land Kenseth a spot with Roush Racing.

"Matt is a very talented race driver," said Martin. "I knew the first time I saw him that he had a great future in the sport. I wanted to do anything I could to help him out."[6]

Martin actually initiated contact with Kenseth. After a drivers' meeting at Talladega in 1997, Martin made his way over to Kenseth and introduced himself. The two chatted, and a lifelong friendship was started.

"The following Monday he called me and said he wanted to sign me up with Roush and wanted to try to do something for the future to help my path to Winston Cup progress a little faster than it

DID YOU KNOW?

In 1997, despite making only twenty-one starts out of thirty Busch races, Kenseth placed second in the rookie standings.

would without (his) help,"
Kenseth said.[7]

Kenseth has leaned
on Martin, learning as
much as he can from the
veteran driver.

DID YOU KNOW?

Before joining Reiser Enterprises in April 1997, Kenseth was second in the ASA series points standings.

"Mark has really guided
my career," Kenseth said. "He
helped me get where I am today,
and I'll always appreciate it. It seems unbelievable that
things have moved this fast, and it's all because of
Mark's help."[8]

The two enjoy such a close relationship that
Martin likes watching Kenseth succeed on the track
nearly as much as he likes to win himself. It was hard
to tell who was more excited about Kenseth's first
Busch victory in 1998—Martin or Kenseth.

"When Matt won his first Busch race at
Rockingham in 1998, that was a tremendous thrill for
me," Martin said. "It was also a big relief. I stepped out
on a limb based on a hunch and convinced Jack that
he could be a big part of Roush Racing's future."[9]

Martin was nearly as ecstatic with Kenseth's
first Winston Cup win in 2000 at the Coca-Cola 600
during Kenseth's rookie season. The Coca-Cola 600
is always one of the toughest races of the season,
and Martin was impressed with Kenseth's ability to
maintain his focus throughout the race.

"There is no better way to get your first win than to do something nobody else has accomplished," Martin said. "That was just the way I had hoped to see it go down. Matt ran a brilliant race. I'm just happy to have had a small part in it."[10]

Martin has even found time to praise Kenseth after his own victories. Martin won at Dover in September 1999, a race in which Kenseth, who raced in five Winston Cup events that year, finished fourth. After the race, Martin was offering praise from the winner's circle.

"You know, I'm just glad to get this win because I don't know how many more of them I'm going to be able to get with (Kenseth) out there," Martin said. "He's spectacular."[11]

At that point, Kenseth had signed a deal to join Roush Racing on the Winston Cup circuit for the 2000 season. Kenseth earned the deal, showing what he could do on the Busch circuit from 1997 to 1999 and his few opportunities in Winston Cup races in 1999. But Martin did his part in making sure Kenseth would land with Roush Racing and not with another team.

DID YOU KNOW?

Since 1998, Kenseth has won twenty-three Busch races and finished in the top ten in 144 of 200 races. Of his wins, three have come at both Fontana and Bristol. He also has a Nextel Cup win at Fontana and two Nextel Cup victories at Bristol.

"Matt has got great instincts for being a racecar driver," Roush said. "He attracted the attention of Mark for having the 'right stuff' and having a thought process that was good."[12]

If there was ever any doubt about how big an influence Martin has been for Kenseth, 1999 is proof. Kenseth ran in five Winston Cup races that year.

DID YOU KNOW?

After seven years as members of Roush Racing, Kenseth had to watch his mentor and friend Mark Martin leave Roush and join Ginn Racing, which would allow Martin to run a Nextel Cup schedule.

However, he had planned to try to enter more races in an effort to make his transition to a full-time Winston Cup schedule easier. But Kenseth talked to Martin first. Based on Martin's advice, Kenseth decided to compete for another full Busch schedule in 1999.

"In my heart, I knew I needed another year (of Busch experience), but you can never get somewhere too fast I don't think," said Kenseth. "You do need experience, but in my mind I always want to do it now. I'm not a patient person.

"I'm not driven by money. I'm driven by winning races. Mark told me that winning races was what Roush Racing was all about. I trust in Mark and believe everything he has told me."[13]

A FUTURE STAR IS BORN

Entering the 1998 Busch season, Reiser Enterprises was on the brink of falling apart. With Kraft pulling its sponsorship at the end of the 1997 season, the team was left scrambling for sponsors and securing money to compete. Once again, Kenseth had to clear more hurdles if his racing career was to take off.

Reiser was able to secure a one-race sponsorship from Lycos for the season opener at Daytona. Kenseth did the rest on the track. After qualifying seventh for the NAPA Auto Parts 300, the young driver stayed clear of trouble throughout the race and finished sixth. The result proved Kenseth could handle himself on the track. More important, it earned him more than $31,000 in prize money, allowing the team to show up for the GM Goodwrench Service Plus 200 the next weekend in Rockingham.

There was Kenseth, wearing a plain blue driver's suit for most of the weekend, absent of corporate logos that often adorn the suits of drivers. Kenseth's car still displayed the Lycos name, but there was no actual sponsorship deal with the company. Reiser kept the decals on in hopes of attracting Lycos to become a permanent sponsor, saying it was the only option he had.

The weekend did not start well for Kenseth. He struggled in qualifying, placing twenty-seventh and forcing him to start the race in the middle of the field. But what a race he would run the following day.

"It's probably a day that we'll never forget because it'll never happen again," said Reiser. "It's a day I don't think you can even put into words. Incredible."[1]

DID YOU KNOW?

Matt Kenseth's sixth-place finish in his first Winston Cup race in 1998 was the third-best showing by a rookie driver. Only Terry Labonte and Rusty Wallace had higher finishes the first time they entered a Winston Cup race since the modern era began in 1972.

THE PERFORMANCE OF A LIFETIME

When the green flag dropped, Kenseth immediately started moving up through the field, passing one car after another. After an accident and one final restart with forty-one laps remaining, Kenseth stood in third place. He trailed only Tony Stewart and Elliott Sadler.

Soon enough, Kenseth zoomed past Sadler, leaving only Stewart ahead of him. The two battled each other the rest of the race, though it looked as if Kenseth was going to finish second after being caught in slow traffic.

But with less than two laps remaining, Kenseth was right behind Stewart, an experienced driver who won a title in the Indy Racing League. Showing the nerve of a veteran, Kenseth gently bumped Stewart from behind and then shot past him. Just like that, Stewart, who had held the lead for sixty laps, was in second place as Kenseth crossed the finish line first. Kenseth led the race for a grand total of one lap and won by .092 seconds.

"We were both running for our first Busch Grand National victory," said Stewart about Kenseth's bump-and-run move. "I didn't do a very good job of getting through (turns) 3 and 4, the last corner of the last lap, and he gave me a little nudge. He could have hit me hard enough to crash me, and he didn't. He just barely nudged me up and out of the way."[2]

Even now, when asked about some of his favorite racing memories, Kenseth recalls his first win at Rockingham.

"Our first Busch win at Rockingham in 1998 (stands out)," Kenseth said. "We were there with Reisers, and we didn't have a sponsor, and we went there and won the race in jeans and t-shirts. I had a generic uniform that was three sizes too small, and I beat guys like Jeff Burton (who finished fourth) and Mark Martin (who placed third), so that is probably my most exciting moment."[3]

The victory made a lasting memory for Kenseth, but it also may have saved his racing career. After a wild celebration in Victory Lane, the good news continued later in the week when Lycos decided to sign on as a sponsor for the rest of the 1998 season. The deal gave the Reiser team security the rest of the year and eased the pressure of racing for survival every week.

THE START OF AN OUTSTANDING SEASON

Kenseth was unable to follow his Rockingham victory with solid results the next two weekends. He placed twenty-fourth in Las Vegas and thirty-third at Nashville. Then followed a string of successes on the track.

During the next eight races, the twenty-six-year-old posted seven top-ten finishes, including a streak of five straight top-ten showings. At the Diamond Hill

Plywood 200 at Darlington, Kenseth came in fourth. Kenseth had a third-place finish the following week at Bristol, an eighth-place finish at Fort Worth, and a fifth-place run at Hickory. Kenseth capped his streak of top-ten finishes with an eighth-place showing at Talladega.

After a "bad" week at Loudon in which he finished sixteenth, Kenseth was back in form at Nazareth, placing fourth. The following week he came in fifth at Charlotte in the CarQuest Auto Parts 300. In that race he held the lead for twenty-five laps, but in the end he was unable to hold off his mentor, Mark Martin.

Success continued for Kenseth. He claimed the checkered flag in the Lycos.com 250 at Pikes Peak. Kenseth claimed pole position for the race and held the lead for 104 of the 250 laps. He then placed in the top ten in seven of the next ten races. Then came a weekend in which he showed everyone he was ready to become a future star in the sport.

BREAKING OUT

In September 1998, Kenseth burst onto the racing scene thanks to a spectacular weekend at the Dover Downs International Speedway. Not only did Kenseth run in the Busch race, the MBNA Gold 200, on Saturday, he also raced in the Winston Cup race on Sunday, filling in for Bill Elliott.

On Saturday, Kenseth dominated the field. Starting fourth, he wasted little time in claiming the lead. Once he got it, he did not relinquish it. He led for 158 laps. The win pulled Kenseth to within 97 points of Earnhardt, Jr., in the Busch standings. Earnhardt, Jr., who was having an outstanding season as well, had 3,766 points to Kenseth's 3,669 with five races remaining.

After claiming the win on Saturday, Kenseth was right back on the racetrack on Sunday for the MBNA Gold 400. Starting sixteenth in a field of forty-three cars, Kenseth showed everyone what he could do on the highest level of NASCAR racing by placing sixth behind racing greats Martin, Jeff Gordon, Jeremy Mayfield, Bobby Labonte, and Rusty Wallace.

"For as young as he is and for his knowledge of racecars, he's the next Jeff Gordon," said Mike Beam, Elliott's team manager. "He knows these racecars from end to end, and he even builds his own shocks.

THEY SAID IT

"I 'bout fell out the booth that day. He ran every bit as well as Bill Elliott did in Bill's car the first time out, and he was every bit as competitive."

— Buddy Baker, The Nashville Network race commentator, describing Matt Kenseth's sixth-place finish in his first Winston Cup race in 1998

A FRIENDLY RIVALRY

During the 1998 and 1999 Busch seasons, Matt Kenseth and Dale Earnhardt, Jr. were rivals on the track. They also were two of the most dominant drivers. Earnhardt won back-to-back points titles those years while Kenseth came in second and third.

But away from the track, the rivalry was pushed aside. The two drivers had developed a friendship.

"He admired my father," Earnhardt, Jr. said. "That's the man that he really appreciated, and I find something comfortable in that fact. That's the reason we became friends. . . . I thought, well, maybe he and I could become good buddies because there really wasn't anybody I knew other than Tony (Eury Jr.) and the guys that I was racing with."

The friendship is somewhat surprising, considering the advantages Earnhardt, Jr. has had in getting his career started compared to Kenseth. Earnhardt, Jr. had the backing of the well-funded Dale Earnhardt, Inc. Kenseth, meanwhile, was scrambling for funds during the 1998 season before his breakout performance landed Reiser Racing some sponsors for the 1999 season.

"I think Matt has always wanted kind of what Dale Jr. had . . . very good equipment in the Busch series and a name to go off of," said Kenseth's wife, Katie. "Matt came from a totally different background. Not that Dale didn't have to work for it, but from Matt's perspective, I think it looked easy."

Despite their different backgrounds, Kenseth has not let the advantages Earnhardt, Jr. may have had come between the two. Kenseth likes Earnhardt, Jr. for the person he is.

"When I look at Matt and he looks at me, it's just dude to dude," Earnhardt, Jr. said. "Matt's one of the few people who doesn't see that (superstar) side of it. He doesn't care. It doesn't matter to him. It's been a great friendship."

Dale Earnhardt, Jr. talks with Matt Kenseth during a break in practice at Lowe's Motor Speedway.

He's not one of your run-of-the-mill people. I'm really impressed with him."[4]

Kenseth's run was one of the best ever by a first-time Winston Cup driver. Only two drivers, Terry Labonte and Wallace, finished better in their debuts since the start of NASCAR's modern era in 1972.

"The kid's got talent, that's for sure," Wallace said. "He's smooth and races clean. I was very comfortable out there racing beside him, and that says a lot for a rookie driver."[5]

Despite all the praise about that weekend, Kenseth remained humble by focusing on the real task at hand. He was already thinking about his next Busch race at Charlotte.

"Sunday was fun, and I gained a lot of experience I know I'll be thankful for in the future," Kenseth said. "But right now, focusing on the next Busch race at Charlotte is what's most important."[6]

With the Busch championship on the line, the battle between Earnhardt, Jr. and Kenseth went down to the wire. Kenseth finished second at Charlotte, but Earnhardt, Jr. was third and claimed the same number of points as Kenseth.

The following week at Gateway, Kenseth came in second again. However, Earnhardt, Jr. won the race to increase his lead to 102 points. Then came a disastrous race at Rockingham. Starting second, Kenseth's car had trouble throughout the race, and he crossed the finish line in twenty-seventh while Earnhardt, Jr. was fourteenth, allowing him to build a 146-point lead over Kenseth.

Kenseth rebounded the following week at Atlanta, placing fourth, but Earnhardt did even better with a second-place showing and held an insurmountable 166-point lead entering the final race of the year at Homestead.

The final race of the season proved interesting. Earnhardt, Jr. suffered engine problems and lasted only 89 laps before leaving the race, resulting in a forty-second place finish. Kenseth, meanwhile, was trying to end the season with a flourish and nearly did so as he placed fourth, ending the year only forty-eight points behind Earnhardt, Jr. for the Busch title.

While Kenseth just missed winning a Busch title, his outstanding season opened the eyes of sponsors. DeWalt signed on to become the primary sponsor for the 1999 season, and Kraft came back and became an associate sponsor of the team, along with Luxaire. After starting the season in search of sponsors, the year ended with sponsors flocking to the team.

DID YOU KNOW? During his 1998 Busch season, Kenseth finished in the top ten twenty-three times, or 74 percent of the races in which he competed. He placed in the top five in just under 55 percent (seventeen times). Only once did he fail to finish a race.

CONTINUED SUCCESS IN 1999

Kenseth did not let his success go to his head the next season. Just as he did in 1998, he came out firing with back-to-back top-five finishes at Daytona and Rockingham to start the year.

Then came the first series of disappointing finishes. He finished thirtieth at Las Vegas and

Dale Earnhardt, Jr. celebrates in Victory Lane.

twenty-fifth at Atlanta before claiming a win at Darlington. However, that victory did not lead to better finishes the following three weeks. He placed eighteenth, fifteenth, and thirty-fifth.

Kenseth turned his season around at Talladega, finishing fourth in the Touchstone Energy 300. The following week, he won the Auto Club 300 at Fontana. Then came an eighth-place finish at Loudon and a third-place showing at Richmond. He followed that by winning the First Union 200 at Nazareth.

Kenseth's success continued the rest of the year. He earned one more win at Bristol and would place in the top ten eleven times. By the end of the season, Kenseth claimed four victories, fourteen top-five finishes, and twenty top-ten finishes.

However, Earnhardt, Jr. was just a little better. He won six races, had eighteen top-five finishes, and twenty-two top-ten finishes to claim the Busch title once again with 4,647 points. Kenseth was third with 4,327 points.

Kenseth knew the time had come to move on to Winston Cup. He was more than ready for the jump, and Roush Racing had a spot for him for the 2000 season. Reiser knew Kenseth was ready as well.

"He's gotten the experience from the Busch series racing against Junior for the championship two years over there," Reiser said. "Maybe the pressure isn't as great there (on the Busch circuit), but it's probably gotten him ready for what he's getting into as we go down the road.

"I think Matt has been able to handle any situation we've had."[7]

THE SOPHOMORE SLUMP

Coming off his Rookie of the Year campaign in 2000, Kenseth and the rest of the DeWalt crew were excited about the start of the 2001 season. Kenseth and his team worked hard in the offseason to get ready. Expectations were high.

"This DeWalt Racing team did some fine-tuning during the off-season," Kenseth said. "We placed a lot of focus on the engine department in order to find more horsepower; practicing pit stops to be more efficient; and the body shop to improve overall aerodynamics."[1]

If the No. 17 car performed as expected, Kenseth had no doubts he would have a successful 2001 season and avoid the dreaded "sophomore jinx," a slump some drivers experience in their second years. "I'm not a superstitious person. I don't believe in the jinx," he said.[2]

OFF TO A ROCKY START

The season began with the Daytona 500. Everyone had high hopes as the race neared, including Kenseth. In qualifying, Kenseth posted the sixteenth best time, an improvement of eight spots from 2000.

Kenseth looked competitive at the start of the race. But at the midway point, the car suffered a broken shock pin, forcing Kenseth to pit and putting the team a few laps down. The setback was too much for Kenseth to overcome. He finished twenty-first.

Kenseth said his showing was decent considering the problems he had with the car. He carried that bit of optimism into the Dura Lube 400 at Rockingham.

That optimism quickly faded as the week progressed. Kenseth struggled during qualifying and started the race, which was delayed more than an hour by rain, thirty-eighth on the grid. Kenseth worked his way up to twenty-ninth, but the race was postponed until Monday due to a heavy downpour.

The race restarted on Lap 51, and Kenseth appeared to be running well. However, his race took a turn for the worse when he got debris stuck in his front grill, leading the water temperature in his car to become hot.

Forced to pit, Kenseth got fresh tires and refueled while waiting for the front grill to be cleaned and the water temperature to cool. The delay, however, dropped him several laps off the leaders. Once back on the track, Kenseth's car was one of the fastest out there. However, he was too far behind the leaders and placed twenty-eighth.

"I'm pretty disappointed about today," Kenseth said. "We had a competitive top-10 car coming into this race, but early in the day we got a piece of debris from another car on our grill and that just hurt our chances for a good finish. The car got hot so fast we had to pit and lost a few laps.

"I was running as fast as the leaders but we could not get those laps back. Our goal then became to finish this race."[3]

During the next five races, his best showing was a fourteenth-place finish at Bristol in the Food City 500.

Not only was Kenseth struggling on race day, he was also struggling during qualification. During that five-week span after Rockingham, his best starting position was twenty-second at Las Vegas. His other starting positions were thirty-eighth, thirtieth, twenty-fourth, and twenty-seventh.

WHAT, ME WORRY?

Kenseth was not the only driver to struggle in 2001. It seemed the entire Roush stable of drivers had a hard time winning. But 2002 saw improvement from the entire team, most notably Kenseth.

The success in 2002 relieved a worried Roush, who wondered if it was perhaps time to get out of racing.

"It feels like 2001 should have been," he said. "I'm relieved that the process that we have—and our structure and our morals and all the things that wind up holding our world together—is working this year, and I don't have to retire. I can keep doing this a while."

TURNING THINGS AROUND?

After finishing twentieth at the Harrah's 500 in Fort Worth, Kenseth headed to Martinsville.

Kenseth experienced little trouble on the track and came in sixth, his best showing of the year. It vaulted him to seventeenth in the points standings.

Unfortunately, the next two weeks, at Talladega and Fontana, were not as good. Kenseth finished nineteenth and seventeenth. But Kenseth was back in the top ten the following week at Richmond, when he placed eighth in the Pontiac Excitement 400. The showing allowed Kenseth to move up to eleventh in the points race, his highest position of the season.

Kenseth, Reiser, and the rest of the DeWalt crew believed they were ready to turn the corner. Reality, however, would prove to be different.

He placed outside the top ten in his next three races before putting on an amazing driving display at Pocono. Qualifying thirty-first, the car handled great throughout the race. Kenseth put his drafting skills to good use as he vaulted toward the front of the field and eventually placed sixth.

But during the next fifteen races, Kenseth crossed the finish line tenth or better only twice. Five times he came in thirty-second or worse, and he did not finish four races due to crashes or trouble with the car.

Kenseth still stood in the top twenty in the points standings, but he was not pleased with how his season was going.

"It was aggravating," said Kenseth. "We couldn't run in the top 20 to save our lives."[4]

Even more aggravating was the fact neither Kenseth nor Reiser could figure out how to improve his performance.

DID YOU KNOW?

Since joining the Cup circuit on a full-time basis in 2000, Kenseth has won at least one Cup race every year except for 2001.

"I never really doubted I could drive the cars when they got them right. I just doubted my ability to figure out what was wrong with our cars because we were running so bad, and we were so far off that I couldn't tell them what to put in the car to make it better," Kenseth said. "That part I doubted. Our team morale, considering how bad we ran, stayed pretty good. Morale is going to get down when you run bad, and there's absolutely nothing you can do about it. If I'm smiling at the shop and at the racetrack, I'll go home when I'm running bad and be miserable. It's tough to keep your chin up."[5]

By the end of the year, Kenseth failed to win a race and had only four top-five finishes and nine top-ten finishes. Interestingly, those numbers were similar to his 2000 results, when he had one victory and eleven top-ten finishes. In fact, Kenseth finished thirteenth in the points race, one spot higher than in 2000. Considering the high expectations Kenseth had entering the 2001 season, the year was a disappointment for him.

"When I came here in '99 and ran my five-race deal, we ran really well in the five races," Kenseth said. "We didn't finish great in all of them but we ran pretty well, and it really wasn't much harder than the Busch series for us to run well right away. I was feeling good about life.

"Mark, in '98, won seven races and was second in points. Everything looked good. Everything looked like it was going to be great, and my rookie year started out really strong, started out really, really good."[6]

Reiser made minor improvements to the car toward the end of the 2001 season, and a team meeting in August helped everyone talk about the problems

Kenseth runs behind a pace car at the start of a race.

and concentrate on a strong finish.

"Everybody was . . . trying to find the easy fix," Reiser said. "We were trying to do too much, trying too hard to change this thing around, and we weren't taking a direction.

"It was a whole group that said, 'We've got to sit down and talk about this.' We discussed a few things, changed our approach a little on how we went to the racetrack and how we approached practice. And slowly, slowly as the year progressed, we got better."[7]

The team was significantly better during the final six races of the season as Kenseth finished in the top-ten four times and had three fourth-place finishes.

Surprisingly, the 2001 season proved to be beneficial to Kenseth. Accustomed to success, his troubles on the track forced him to race with the rest of the field. It forced Kenseth to really learn how to race.

"This sounds dumb, but, to tell you the truth, the most intense racing that I've done was probably last year running in the back," Kenseth said. "Running in the back is really, really hard. When you're back there fighting for twentieth and your car is handling terrible and you're fighting your car like crazy and you're trying to pass cars and get the best finish you can, it's really tough.

"When your car is handling good and you can run up front and you can pass cars and you catch them and try to figure out how to get around them, that's when it's fun. That's when it's maybe not as difficult, but it's difficult when your car is not handling good and you don't have the equipment underneath you to do as good as you think you can do and you're overdriving all the time to try to make the car go faster. That's the most intense racing you'll do. The most intense racing happens from about nineteenth to twenty-seventh."[8]

A BETTER SEASON

The team decided to put 2001 behind them and concentrate on 2002, using the strong finish as a good starting point. However, Kenseth was not happy with the start of the campaign after finishing thirty-third in the season-opening Daytona 500.

The season took a turn for the better the following week at the Subway 400 in Rockingham. After qualifying twenty-fifth, Kenseth blew through the field and held the lead for 152 laps. He was in a tight battle with Sterling Marlin and Bobby Labonte before slipping past them into first place with six laps remaining. A caution flag came out with five laps remaining, and Kenseth won the race under yellow.

After the race, Kenseth praised his pit crew for helping him secure his second career victory and first in more than a year.

"They (the crew) did it today," Kenseth said. "They got me out front every time. When I was behind, even if my car was handling good, I couldn't do anything with them. When we were up front, we could drive away from them. It was a great effort for the guys."[9]

Kenseth drove to top-ten finishes in five of the following six races. After

CONCENTRATING ON THE WINSTON CUP

Throughout his career, Kenseth has often raced in Busch events when they are held at the same track as a Cup race. However, in an effort to improve his results on the Cup circuit in 2002 after struggling the previous year, Kenseth entered only four Busch races that season. His results were good. He had one top-five finish and two top-ten showings.

finishing fourteenth at Las Vegas, he came in fourth, eighth, and sixth in the following three events. Kenseth then secured his second win of the season at the Samsung/RadioShack 500 in Fort Worth. Then came a second-place finish the following week at Martinsville.

What a difference one year can make. Through the first eight races in 2001, Kenseth did not have a single victory, failed to finish in the top ten, and was standing in seventeenth in the points standings. Through the first eight

Kenseth holds up the trophy in Victory Lane after winning the 2002 Subway 400.

races in 2002, Kenseth was in second place in the standings thanks to two victories, three top-five finishes, and five top-ten finishes.

Then came another series of finishes that alternated between good and bad. After finishing

NEW CAREER HIGHS

One key to Kenseth's turnaround in 2002 was his average starting position compared to 2001. During the 2001 season, Kenseth's average starting position was twenty-eighth, leading to an average finish of nineteenth. But Kenseth improved his qualifying times throughout the 2002 season, leading to an average starting spot of eighteenth. His average finish was just under sixteenth.

STEADY IMPROVEMENT

By finishing eighth in the Cup standings in 2002, Kenseth enjoyed a third straight year in which he showed improvement. He finished fourteenth in 2000 and thirteenth in 2001.

second at Martinsville, Kenseth was thirtieth and twentieth in his next two races before placing sixth and second in the following two races.

Kenseth eventually notched his third win of the year by claiming the Sirius Satellite Radio 400 at Michigan. But during the next ten races, Kenseth finished thirtieth or worse five times while finishing in the top ten four times.

After struggling at Darlington with a thirty-seventh-place showing, Kenseth rebounded at Richmond the following weekend by winning the

Kenseth's car is serviced by his crew.

Chevrolet Monte Carlo 400. Kenseth finished with five wins, the most on the Winston Cup circuit. However, he also finished thirtieth or worse eleven times and did not finish a race three times. The inconsistency resulted in an eighth-place finish in the points standings.

"I wish we had more consistency and contended for the title," Kenseth said. "But I can't complain. I can't go back and say, 'That (stinks),' and wish we did something better. I don't think there was anybody, including us, who expected to win five races and be as competitive as we were."[10]

Carrying a positive attitude entering the 2003 Winston Cup season, an energized Kenseth was excited to be back at the Daytona 500. The 2002 season ended on a relatively strong note, and the DeWalt team was confident it could build on that success.

The week started well as Kenseth had a third-place finish in the Budweiser Shootout. However, the team suffered a bump in the road during qualifying, forcing Kenseth to a thirty-sixth-place starting position. But with his car running well throughout the practice sessions, Kenseth was not too worried about his place on the grid. Soon after the green flag dropped, Kenseth was zipping in and out of traffic. By the fiftieth lap, Kenseth was running in sixth place.

Then came some bad luck. An accident near the pit road wall kept Kenseth from entering pit road. Rain then began to fall, and the race was red-flagged, or stopped. The delay lasted for an hour before racing resumed. Having to pit after racing resumed, Kenseth dropped to thirteenth.

Then came another crash on the track. Many of the drivers opted to pit, but not Kenseth. Believing more rain was on the way, he gambled and stayed on the track. The move seemed to work as he moved all the way to fourth place.

But the expected rain did not come. Kenseth was forced to pit. The pit stop lasted only fourteen seconds, but that was long enough to see Kenseth fall to twenty-fourth. He finished twentieth.

"We were getting better fuel mileage than most, so we could have run to about Lap 104," Kenseth said. "The caution came out on Lap 97 for that crash, and we were just hoping to stay out and that it would rain and we'd be able to get a better finish out of it. We were running 19th and there were only 30 cars on the lead lap, so I figured it was a gamble worth taking. It didn't really work out because we got back to 20th, but it was worth a try."[1]

Race week at Rockingham the following weekend went much better for Kenseth. He qualified eighteenth for the Subway 400, and much as he did at Daytona, he quickly dashed toward the front of the field. Unlike Daytona, Kenseth was able to stay near the front of the field and finished third.

He improved on that finish at Las Vegas. While his qualifying run for the UAW-DaimlerChrysler 400 was not spectacular, it was good enough for a seventeenth-place start. From the outset, Kenseth loved the way his car handled and stuck to the track while banking through the turns.

Everything about the setup of the car was to his liking, and it showed. Kenseth swiftly passed one driver after another, and by Lap 172, Kenseth was in the lead. He dominated the field the rest of the race on his way to his first win of 2003.

"I'm really proud of this team. We made a few changes to the crew during the off-season, and for them to perform like they did today is just a testament to how hard they work and how dedicated they are," Kenseth said.[2]

Kenseth was now in second place in the points standings, trailing Michael Waltrip by only three points. It would not be long before Kenseth took over the top spot in the standings. In fact, it took only one week.

LEADING THE PACK

The next race on the schedule was the Bass Pro Shops MBNA 500 in Atlanta. Racing a car that was running better than ever, Kenseth placed fourth, earning him 160 points and vaulting him to the top of the points race with 618, forty-nine better than Tony Stewart.

Kenseth would never relinquish his role as points leader the rest of the season, spanning a record thirty-three straight weeks. Week after week, Kenseth turned in one strong performance after another.

He was eighth at Darlington, second at Bristol, sixth at Fort Worth, and ninth at Talladega before finally finishing out of the top ten at Martinsville, when he came in twenty-second. It did not take long for Kenseth to get back into the top ten, however.

The following week at Fontana, Kenseth came in ninth. Ensuing finishes were seventh at Richmond, second at Charlotte, seventh at Dover, third at Pocono, and fourth at Michigan. Fifteen races into the season, Kenseth was the model of consistency.

Only twice did he fail to secure a top-ten finish. Seven times he finished fifth or better. From the time

ALMOST HOME
The Chicagoland Speedway is the closest track on the Nextel Cup circuit to Cambridge, Wisconsin, Kenseth's hometown.

Kenseth swings wide to avoid a crash during the Checker Auto Parts 500.

he took over the points lead after Atlanta to his fourth-place finish in Michigan, his lead in the standings grew from forty-nine to 185 points.

Kenseth gained more confidence with each passing week. That confidence was noticed by Geoff Smith, the president of Roush Racing.

"Over time, I've seen how the pressure of success can detract from the mission, but I just don't

see that in Matt," Smith said. "He's the kind of guy who says, 'What are we going to do this week? Did we do it? OK, let's work on it next week.'

"I think the longer the season goes with Matt at the front, the tougher it's going to be to be thrown off base. Every week they get more confidence in the quality of their program."[3]

During a five-week span from June 22 to July 27, Kenseth was in and out of the top ten. He placed sixth at Pepsi 400 in Daytona and third at Loudon

TURN IT UP!

Kenseth's favorite band is Metallica. During the summer of 2003, he and his wife, Katie, went to a concert and met everyone in the band except Lars Ulrich, an ironic twist since Kenseth named one of his cats Lars, after the band's drummer.

but was fourteenth at Sonoma, twelfth at Chicago, and thirteenth at Pocono. Despite the up-and-down finishes during this stretch of the season, Kenseth's lead in the points race grew to 232. His lead increased despite the fact he was not winning races—proving consistency is just as important as wins.

"It's still really important (to win) and has a lot of significance, but I think more people are looking toward a championship," Kenseth said. "The main reason I say that is because last year we were able to win five races and had a great year, especially compared to 2001, but the last three weeks with me leading the points I've probably done more interviews than I did the whole year last year winning five races."[4]

AIMING FOR THE TITLE

With sixteen weeks left in the season, the field had time to catch Kenseth. But when looking at the tracks the circuit was going to race on the rest of the season, Kenseth was in a great position to succeed. He had top-ten finishes at three of the tracks in 2002. And while he had struggled at Watkins Glen and Homestead in the past, the DeWalt team was confident it could solve the tracks in 2003.

"I hope we can keep doing it. All you can do is show up every week and do the best job you can," said Kenseth. "All you can do is go and run as hard as you can every week and try to gather as many points as you can and see how it shakes out at the end of the year. We're not doing anything different than we ever did. Things are just falling into place more than what maybe they have in the past."[5]

After his thirteenth-place showing at Pocono, Kenseth drove the No. 17 car to four straight top-ten finishes before coming in fourteenth at Darlington.

After Darlington, Kenseth bounced right back, continuing his relentless march toward a Winston Cup championship by finishing seventh, seventh, and

MORE COOKIES PLEASE

Kenseth cannot get enough oatmeal chocolate chip cookies. Whenever he returns to Cambridge to visit his family, his mother always bakes his favorite cookies. Kenseth will then sit around with his family and friends and eat all the cookies he can.

ninth at Richmond, Loudon, and Dover. With eight weeks left in the season, Kenseth held a season-high 436-point lead over the rest of the Winston Cup field. It was a lead that would prove to be insurmountable despite Kenseth stumbling a bit down the stretch.

Kenseth was forced to leave the race at Talladega with engine trouble, giving him a thirty-third-place finish. The following week at Kansas he finished thirty-sixth after suffering a crash.

Kenseth's lead shrank to 259 points due to those back-to-back finishes at Talladega and Kansas. But Kenseth had no reason to be worried about losing his lead.

He finished eighth at Charlotte, thirteenth at Martinsville, and eleventh at Atlanta. The circuit then headed to Phoenix, where Kenseth came in sixth to take a 228-point lead into the second-to-last race of the year at Rockingham, which was one of Kenseth's favorite tracks.

Starting with the second race there in 2001, Kenseth finished tenth, first, eighth, and then third earlier in 2003 at the track. Once again, the track proved to Kenseth's liking. He came in fourth. The showing was not only his eleventh top-five finish of the year, it clinched the Winston Cup title for Kenseth with one race remaining.

"It's unbelievable. This is beyond my wildest dreams," Kenseth said. "I never thought I'd ever have

Matt Kenseth kisses his wife, Katie, after winning the 2003 NASCAR Winston Cup Championship.

the opportunity to sit in one of these cars, much less be the champion. I'm just so appreciative to my team, my owners, my sponsors, everybody that puts this thing together. I'm pretty lucky. There are thousands of racecar drivers out there that I'm sure could do a better job than I have and not many people get this opportunity. I'm just thankful to be in good equipment with good people working on it."[6]

The season-ending race at Homestead did not finish as Kenseth had hoped. His car's engine blew on the twenty-eighth lap, leaving him with a last-place finish and 5,022 points for the year. Because of the engine failure, the final margin of victory over Jimmie Johnson was only 90 points, but that did not really show just how good Kenseth had been the entire season.

Kenseth hoists his championship trophy.

Kenseth won only one race all year, but he had eleven top-five finishes. He finished in the top ten in 70 percent of his outings. While his average starting position was only twenty-first, his average finish was tenth. Only twice did he not finish a race.

"Matt was like a machine," said driver Jimmie Johnson. "He

knew the system. He kept piling up the points and staying away from trouble."[7]

CHANGING RULES

Kenseth is not the first driver to win the points title with only one victory. Benny Parsons did so in 1973. Three drivers have won titles with only two wins during the season. Terry Labonte accomplished that feat twice.

Still, after Kenseth's title run, changes were made to the points system and, more important, a ten-race playoff—"The Chase for the Cup"—was

DID YOU KNOW? After clinching the Winston Cup title, it did not take long for Kenseth to start to hear praise from all corners. He faced the media in Chicago during a news conference, and Wisconsin Governor Jim Doyle declared the Monday after Kenseth's title-clinching run at the Pop Secret 400 as "Matt Kenseth Day."

created, coinciding with a name change from Winston Cup to Nextel Cup. Many have attributed the scoring change directly to Kenseth and his title run.

Kenseth, however, does not worry about any changes to the scoring system. In the end, he said his performance during the season spoke for itself.

"You know, last year we won five races, which was the most in the series last year, and finished eighth in the points," said Kenseth. "This year we won one race, but we were really, really consistent, and I think we had, statistically, a really great season. We had more

A VISIT WITH THE PRESIDENT

With the Winston Cup title came a lot of attention for Kenseth. One of his biggest thrills was getting an opportunity to meet President George Bush at the White House. Bush honored Kenseth for his championship along with NASCAR's top-ten drivers during a fifteen-minute ceremony. In typical Kenseth fashion, he said the meeting "was really cool."

points than the champion had last year by at least a couple hundred, even though we were the first car out at Homestead.

"I feel like we've done a good job of being consistent and running up front. There's a lot of different ways of looking at it. In football, if you look at wins, there's two teams—one winner and one loser. In racing, there's one guy who's the winner on Sunday and there's forty-two guys who didn't win. So, we ran up at the front of our class, I feel like, all year long."[8]

Kenseth gives President George W. Bush a NASCAR jacket.

MATT KENSETH, THE COMMON MAN

Since joining the Cup circuit in 2000, Kenseth has earned the respect of his fellow drivers. He has won a Cup title and was Rookie of the Year.

Yet Kenseth is still an unknown racer in many American homes. Diehard NASCAR fans know who he is, but few others would be able to identify him if he were standing in the same room. One of the reasons for that, however, is the fact Kenseth seldom seeks attention.

Kenseth is so humble and unassuming, he does not even have a glitzy place to display his Winston Cup championship trophy. According to Kenseth, it is just sitting on the kitchen counter.

"He doesn't want to be a TV star," said Ricky Rudd, a longtime NASCAR driver. "I guess that's the exception in this day and age. He's kind of a throwback to the day when you did your talking on the track."[1]

During prerace festivities, autograph hunters are often walking around. Jeff Gordon is a popular driver, as are Earnhardt, Jr., Tony Stewart, and Jimmie Johnson. Despite being a Cup champion, Kenseth often goes unnoticed.

"Sometimes we'll go places and people will ask, 'Are you Matt?' and when he answers yes, they'll say, 'I thought so, because I recognize your wife,'" said Katie Kenseth. "Typically, Matt isn't recognized too much. We can be at dinner with three other drivers and fans will come up and speak to them, and as they're leaving you'll see on their face that they've figured out who Matt is. But that's OK."[2]

Earnhardt, Jr., Kenseth's fellow driver and good friend, has never been camera shy. He said, "I wish I had been a little smarter about it (seeking attention earlier in his career). I should have been a little more private, a little more controlled."[3]

Since their days racing together in the Busch series, Earnhardt, Jr. has always received more attention. One reason for that is because of who

Matt and Katie Kenseth arrive at the 2004 NASCAR
Awards Banquet.

Junior's father was. Kenseth has seen firsthand how
it can be a circus atmosphere wherever Earnhardt,
Jr. is, and Kenseth is happy to be able to enter a
room unnoticed.

"I'll tell you a story. After Darlington (in 2002)
he needed a ride home and asked to ride with me. My
wife, Katie, and I were driving one of Jack's (Roush)

Mustangs down there so we gave him a ride home," Kenseth said. "We stopped at Wendy's to get a bite to eat and went inside to use the bathroom and get some food to go. Everybody in there recognized him and started screaming like we were at a rock concert and they had spotted a rock star.

"Little girls in there were screaming and cornered him and swarmed all around him. Nobody

AN INSPIRED STORY

It is said some of the most passionate fans in sports are NASCAR fans. Kristopher Carro falls into the category of passionate fan and got to meet his hero at Lowe's Motor Speedway after writing a fascinating story.

As one of his class assignments, Carro, then a third-grader, was to write a fictional story. He decided to do an updated version of Cinderella. In his story, "A Modern Cinderella," Carro substituted the pumpkin coach with a Jaguar and Nike Airs replaced the glass slipper.

In the story, Cinderella has to stay behind and clean the house while her stepmother and stepsisters attend the Daytona 500. While cleaning, Cinderella is visited by her fairy godmother, who dresses her in a Matt Kenseth shirt, bell-bottoms, and Nike Airs. Cinderella then heads to the race in her Jaguar and meets Kenseth.

The two go out for dinner and dancing before Cinderella runs off at midnight, leaving her shoes behind. Kenseth searches for Cinderella, and, when he finally finds her, asks her to marry him. They get married on December 4, 2000, the same day as Kenseth's actual wedding day to Katie Kenseth.

even noticed me. I didn't envy him one iota. If it was like that for me every day, it would drive me crazy. It really doesn't bother me at all anymore since that day. I enjoy my time away, and I enjoy being able to go where I want without necessarily being cornered all the time."[4]

Kenseth does his best to avoid crowds. Whenever possible, he heads to his log cabin in Wisconsin, where he and his wife or some old friends from high school will just relax. The nearest grocery store is an hour away.

"It's out in the middle of nowhere. There are no people around, and it's fun to get away and relax," Kenseth said. "No cities. No nothing. I like to do that."[5]

CONNECTING WITH THE FANS

Kenseth's approach to racing and the way he lives his life reflect the midwestern values instilled in him since childhood. His demeanor and his character are why Kenseth has a legion of devoted fans.

"Just because he's good in his personal life and seems to get along with people, the media doesn't want to write about a guy like that," said Kenseth fan Gary Hess of Pittsburgh. "They'd rather focus on bad boys.

"I like that he's a humble person. I like the common man. He's not like Jeff Gordon or someone who thinks they're on a different plateau than the others."[6]

During the Second Annual Matt Kenseth Fan Appreciation Night, nearly 800 fans paid $25 apiece to pack the building where the event was held. While Kenseth was not comfortable being there, it was still something he wanted to do.

The evening was a way to allow fans to get close to their favorite driver. The event also allows Kenseth to remember who he really is and where he came from.

"It's a reality check. He really is one of the best. Sometimes it's hard to comprehend. We look at ourselves as regular people," said Roy Kenseth. "But Matt's feet are on the ground, believe me. He's still basically a shy kid."[7]

One of Kenseth's good friends is Cup driver Jeff Green. He and his wife, Michelle, became good friends with Kenseth and his wife when they were both in the Busch series. Green said people just seem to gravitate to Kenseth because of his character.

"He doesn't want anything from anyone other than to race people fairly," Green said. "If more of the competitors were like that, NASCAR would be a lot better."[8]

DID YOU KNOW?

Kenseth participates in fantasy football and is in the same league as his wife and her sister.

A LIGHTER SIDE

Kenseth's close friends see a person different from the one portrayed by the media. When hanging out with people he is close to, Kenseth likes to pull pranks.

"Among friends, he's kind of the class clown and always fooling around," Reiser said. "But when he gets outside in the public, he shows up for race weekend, and he wants to race.

"He's a very intelligent guy, and he thinks a lot about what he says before he says it. I think that makes a big difference in how he comes across. He's always been that way. He's well-thought-out before he opens his mouth."[9]

During a visit to New York, Kenseth was on the *Live with Regis and Kelly* show. One of the show's bits was to see how many pies Kenseth could throw at Kelly Ripa's face in one minute. Kenseth threw seventeen pies to earn a spot in the *Guinness Book of World Records*. The very next day, Ripa topped Kenseth's record when she threw twenty-four pies at a celebrity.

DID YOU KNOW?

Matt was a member of the Gillette Young Guns in 2004 and 2005. He and fellow NASCAR drivers Kurt Busch, Dale Earnhardt, Jr., Kevin Harvick, Jimmie Johnson, and Ryan Newman teamed with Gillette in a promotion that gave fans and the National Prostate Cancer Coalition the chance to win prizes ranging from $1,000 to $1,000,000.

Kenseth signs an autograph for a fan.

He also appeared on the *Late Show with David
Letterman*. Kenseth fulfilled a lifelong dream as he and
the other Chase drivers took part in Letterman's Top
10 list that night, which was "The top 10 things never
before said by a NASCAR driver."

"It was fun, and I did always want to be on there,
but it wasn't at all what I expected," said Kenseth.
"We had to be there like three hours before, an they
stuck us down in this room in the basement that was
full of pipes. It was supposedly their 'green room,'
but The Rock was also on the show that night, and
he was never in that green room. So basically, we sat
down in this room full of pipes for three hours, then

got to be on the show for one minute, and I never got to meet Letterman. I shook his hand, that was it."[10]

Despite the brief appearance on the show, Kenseth was happy with his line and ability to deliver it with a straight face.

FLYING THE FRIENDLY SKIES

During his childhood in Wisconsin, Kenseth was introduced to the joys of aviation by his grandfather, Helmer. While Kenseth got involved in racing, he never forgot his love of flying.

Because of his profession, Kenseth spends almost as much time in the air flying to tracks as he does racing on the tracks. Thinking it would be better to fly the plane instead of always just riding in one, Kenseth decided to take flying lessons.

"I had and still have a jet, and my pilot, Elwood, is a great pilot," Kenseth said. "But I just sat there in the back and thought, 'Flying's pretty cool, and that would definitely give me something to do other than sit in the back and stare out the window for two or three hours.' I got my pilot's license, instrument rating and recently got my multi-engine rating."[12]

Kenseth now flies himself to several races each year. Having his own license also allows him to fly to Wisconsin to visit his family.

Does Kenseth's family worry about him flying around the country?

"Common sense will tell you that you can get killed ten times as easy on the ground as in the air, but if it happens in the air, everybody hears about it," said Roy Kenseth. "So I'm not worried when he's in his airplane. Now, if you ask me about when he's on a snowmobile or a motorcycle, yeah, that makes me worry."[13]

DID YOU KNOW? **If Kenseth had to stop racing tomorrow, he said he and his wife would probably live in his cabin in Wisconsin and help his son, Ross, with his racing career, or he would become a private pilot.**

SEEKING THE ELUSIVE SECOND TITLE

As the reigning Cup champion, the quiet Kenseth was now considered one of the top drivers in the Nextel Cup field. If living up to high expectations was too much for Kenseth to handle, he did not show it at the start of the 2004 season.

Kenseth finished ninth at the Daytona 500, giving him a positive start to the year. The following week at Rockingham, Kenseth claimed his first victory of the season, despite starting twenty-third. Las Vegas followed, and Kenseth took the checkered flag.

"It's great to come to Vegas. You don't always leave here a winner, so it's fun to come here and leave a winner," Kenseth said.[1]

With two consecutive victories and three straight top-ten finishes, Kenseth found himself atop the standings with 523 points, eighty-eight more than second-place Tony Stewart. Kenseth was feeling good about the start of the season.

"This is a racecar driver's dream come true to come out and win two in a row," Kenseth said.[2]

Kenseth remained strong throughout the season. After the final regular-season race at Richmond, the first Chase for the Cup began with Kenseth sitting in fifth place.

PLAYING NO FAVORITES

Since joining the Nextel Cup circuit full time in 2000, Kenseth has won sixteen races. Those wins have come at ten different tracks. Kenseth holds multiple wins at four tracks, claiming victories at Rockingham, Michigan, Las Vegas, and Bristol twice. Kenseth has experienced the most success at Michigan International Speedway. In seventeen career starts through 2007, he has two wins, seven top-five finishes, and eleven top-ten finishes. His average finish of eighth is the best among any Cup track.

STRUGGLING DOWN THE STRETCH

The Chase started well for Kenseth. He finished second at the Sylvania 300 at Loudon. The finish allowed Kenseth to move into fourth place, only ten points behind leader Earnhardt, Jr.

The strong showing, however, would be the best race Kenseth would have during the Chase. The following week at Dover, Kenseth's day in the MBNA America 400 ended early.

On Lap 119, Kenseth lost control of his car entering pit road. He struck a tire barrier at the pit entrance. The crew was able to repair much of the damage, allowing Kenseth to return to the race. But he lost so much ground he finished thirty-second.

"I thought, really, a right-front tire was starting to go down, and we discussed whether we wanted to pit or not to pit and kind of made a decision that we

Kenseth slams into the barrier at the entrance of pit row.

needed to pit," Kenseth said. "I got it slowed down OK, I thought, and when I got on the apron it looked clean but it was real slick from that other car blowing up earlier, and I just lost control of it."[3]

The poor finish devastated Kenseth's quest for the Cup title. He fell to seventh in the standings. The next four weeks produced only one top-ten finish, dropping Kenseth to ninth in the standings, more than 260 points behind leader Kurt Busch.

Any hopes Kenseth had of staging a miraculous comeback and claiming the title during the final four races of the season ended at the Bass Pro Shops MBNA 500 in Atlanta. Kenseth suffered mechanical failure and finished forty-first.

More frustration followed as engine trouble at Phoenix led to a thirty-sixth-place showing. Kenseth finished the final two weeks of the season placing twentieth at Darlington and nineteenth at Homestead. What started as a strong year ended with an eighth-place finish, 437 points behind Busch. "This was a strange season for me," Kenseth said.[4]

DISAPPOINTING START TO 2005

The 2005 season started the way the 2004 campaign ended—in disappointment. In the season-opener at Daytona, Kenseth suffered engine failure on the thirty-fourth lap, spelling the end of the day for the No. 17 car and resulting in a forty-second-place finish.

The first twelve races of the season were horrific for Kenseth. Only once did he finish in the top ten, placing eighth at Las Vegas in week three. Kenseth thought his season was taking a turn for the better after an eleventh-place finish at Martinsville, but two weeks later he suffered a crash at Phoenix, leaving him in forty-second place.

Overcoming obstacles throughout his career, Kenseth faced one of his toughest challenges yet. His chance of qualifying for the Chase was in jeopardy. He was not even one of the top twenty points earners. Then came a tremendous turnaround.

The next eleven races produced seven top-ten finishes. The surge continued at Bristol, where he won his first race of the season. Amazingly, Kenseth moved into eleventh place in the standings, only eleven points shy of tenth place and a spot in the Chase.

The good times continued at Fontana as Kenseth placed seventh, a result that lifted him into ninth place and on the brink of landing a spot in the Chase with one race to go in the regular season.

LET'S SKIP SONOMA

Kenseth would be more than happy if Sonoma's Infineon Raceway was taken off the schedule. In eight starts there through the 2007 season, he has yet to finish better than fourteenth and has never led a single lap.

Kenseth secured a spot in the Chase for the Cup the following weekend when he placed second at Richmond. The strong showing vaulted Kenseth into eighth place in the standings and gave him a shot of confidence for the start of the Chase.

"We accomplished exactly what we came here to do tonight," Kenseth said. "I can't say enough about this DeWalt team. Not long ago, everyone had pretty much written us off as championship contenders, but these guys never gave up or lost focus and continued to work hard on our cars and our pit stops. We were awesome on pit road tonight."[5]

The momentum continued at the first Chase race at Loudon, where Kenseth placed third in the Sylvania 300.

But the good times came to a sudden end at Dover. After a run of five straight finishes of seventh or better, Kenseth, who experienced tire problems throughout the race, suffered a cut on the right front tire on Lap 367, sending him into the wall. The team tried to repair the damage, but it was too significant and there was not enough time left. Kenseth retired from the race in thirty-fifth place.

Even more damaging was the drop in the standings. Kenseth now was in ninth place, 124 points behind Stewart.

"It just wasn't meant for us today," said Kenseth. "We had a pretty good car that had gotten

Cars race through Turn 2 of the Gatorade Duel #2 in 2005.

better as the day progressed. We battled back from that first tire deal, got our lap back, and were moving forward. It's disappointing, for sure. Everyone knows that there are only eight more races, and each one is so important. But we still have time, and we'll bounce back."[6]

Kenseth did bounce back, finishing third in the UAW-Ford 500 at Talladega and fifth at the Banquet 400 in Kansas. The bad news was he gained only eight points on Stewart and one spot in the standings.

After back-to-back finishes outside the top ten, Kenseth placed fifth at Atlanta and third at Fort Worth to move into sixth place. He trailed Stewart by 135 points, but Kenseth still had a shot at the title.

Whatever hope Kenseth had of winning the title came to an end at the Checker Auto Parts 500 in Phoenix. While running fifth, brake problems devastated Kenseth, and he finished thirty-second.

"It was a disappointing turn of events, for sure," Kenseth said. "It was just a freak thing to happen. We had a problem with the brakes on the left rear. We fixed the problem, but in the process we lost three laps. The car was really good after that, and I really thought we could make up some ground if the cautions had fallen our way.

"They didn't, of course, and we finished way back in the pack and took a hit in the points. Still, we'll head to Homestead and try to finish the season on a high note and gain all the points that we can."[7]

In typical Kenseth fashion, both he and his crew did their best to finish on the high note Kenseth talked about after Phoenix. They lived up to their word as Kenseth finished third and ended the year in seventh place, 181 points behind Stewart.

If there was a silver lining to the end of the season, it was the strong finish at Homestead. Kenseth said it was a good way to end the year and gave everyone on the team a good feeling heading into 2006.

COMING OUT STRONG

The Daytona 500 kicked off the season once again in 2006. Kenseth did not have his best race, finishing fifteenth. But in the next two weeks, he won at Fontana and finished second in Las Vegas.

The two wins were a preview of what was to come. During the next fourteen races, Kenseth notched a win at Dover, racked up eight top-five finishes, and had nine top-ten results overall. After finishing fifth at the Pepsi 400 at Daytona, Kenseth was in second place in the Cup standings, trailing Jimmie Johnson, who would prove to be Kenseth's main rival throughout the season, by only eight points.

Kenseth suffered a stretch in which he had only one top-five showing during a five-week span. But the DeWalt team put together another strong run, starting at Michigan. Qualifying third for the GFS Marketplace 400, Kenseth cruised to his third win of the season.

One week later, Kenseth again was in the winner's circle after emerging victorious at the Sharpie 500 at Bristol. Johnson now held only a seven-point lead over Kenseth. With four wins and thirteen top-five finishes at that point of the campaign, Kenseth said the season was his best yet as a Cup driver.

"If we never win the title again, I'm real thankful for the year we did," Kenseth said. "But I think this is probably our best chance to win one. Our chance is better as far as pure performance when compared to 2003. We're performing at a championship level. That wasn't always the case in 2003."[8]

Kenseth moved atop the points lead the following week by finishing seventh at Fontana. The next week at Richmond, the final race of the regular season, Kenseth drove to an eighth-place finish and was the points leader heading into the Chase.

"I'm excited to go to Loudon with the points lead," Kenseth said. "Our good short track car is sitting at home all ready to go to Loudon, so, overall, I'm pretty happy with the season, and hopefully we'll keep it up."[9]

THE CHASE BEGINS

The weekend at Loudon was disappointing. Kenseth qualified twenty-fifth for the Sylvania 300, not a good position on a track where passing is difficult. Doing his best to pass the cars in the field, Kenseth wound up finishing tenth, dropping him to third in the standings.

Kenseth duplicated his Loudon finish the next week at Dover, lifting him to within eighteen points of first place.

Kenseth then finished twenty-third at Kansas, fourth at Talladega, and fourteenth at Charlotte. After Charlotte, Kenseth was not in the best of spirits despite being only forty-five points out of first place. With only five races remaining, he knew he and the rest of the DeWalt team would have to get better.

"We've had some problems, but we haven't really had the knockout blow by having a fortieth place or blowing an engine or any of that," he said. "We've had our struggles and had a bad finish at Kansas. We didn't do great last week, but we really haven't really had the devastating one (bad finish). We've been hanging in there. We know that we have to do much better than what we've done, but we still feel like we're in it."[10]

A BRIEF RAY OF HOPE

Between the Bank of America 500 at Charlotte and the Subway 500 at Martinsville, Reiser and his crew did all they could to improve the performance of the car. While the No. 17 was not at its best at Martinsville, it was good enough to finish eleventh.

More important, Kenseth left the race in the points lead, taking a thirty-six-point advantage over Kevin Harvick. Kenseth claimed the pole at Atlanta the following week. But on Sunday, his car did not perform as well. Kenseth finished fourth, shrinking his lead to twenty-six points with three races remaining.

"We finished fourth, and we had a forty-fourth-place car, so my team did a great job with it," Kenseth said. "That's how we need to run to have a shot at (the championship). All the rest of those guys are going to be running in the top five, and we need to be there in order to have a shot at it."[11]

THE TITLE SLIPS AWAY

Kenseth was not overly confident heading into the final three races of the year. The car failed to perform at the level it had earlier in the year. Fort Worth was another frustrating race. Kenseth placed twelfth and lost his lead in the standings. Johnson, who finished second, first, and second the three previous weeks, placed second at Fort Worth to take a seventeen-point lead over Kenseth. The former champion was worried heading into the final two races of the season.

"We ran awful all weekend at Texas. We ran awful at Atlanta until the race. We ran hideous at Kansas," Kenseth said. "The only reason we're where we are—let's be realistic—is we haven't broke any parts or haven't crashed. We still have a shot at it, but right now, that's really a stretch the way we're going.

"I really think if we can run in the top five the last two races we have a shot at it (the title). But the way we're running, I'm not sure we can do that."[12]

More problems followed at Phoenix. Kenseth finished thirteenth and left Arizona trailing Johnson by sixty-three points. Kenseth would have to finish at least twelve spots higher than Johnson to win the championship at the season finale at Homestead.

That did not happen. Kenseth finished sixth, but Johnson made sure he stayed out of trouble and monitored Kenseth's position throughout the race. Safely steering his car across the finish line, Johnson finished ninth to claim the Cup title.

Kenseth was disappointed, but he knew he had a good season. He had won four races, his highest total since his five victories in 2002. His fifteen top-five finishes was a career best. Kenseth's average finish and average start were also career highs.

During the season, Kenseth also led a career-high 1,132 laps. In addition, he had finished in the top ten in the points standings five consecutive seasons. Clearly, the future is bright for Kenseth.

"We probably ran on average better than we have any other year," Kenseth said. "We led more laps, and we won some races, and we were in position to win a lot of races."[13]

ANOTHER CHASE IN 2007

Kenseth had yet another solid season in 2007. He won two races and qualified for the Chase for the Nextel Cup once again. His 13 top-five finishes in 2007 ranked third behind Jimmie Johnson and Jeff Gordon. He also ranked in the top five in earnings.

"I think we're probably not one of the favorite two or three teams, we're maybe in that next group after them. I feel good about my team but we're not quite there. Anyone who runs toward the front is close. Winning the Chase really is a matter of doing well on the little things," Kenseth said.[14]

So, just like Kenseth figured, he was in seventh place following the first Chase race. He spent the next seven races fluctuating between tenth and last place. A second-place finish in the Dickies 500 at Texas Motor

Kenseth celebrates in Victory Lane on February 22, 2004.

Speedway, the second-to-last race of the season, catapulted him up to sixth place in the Chase for the Cup. Kenseth then ended the season in style, winning the Ford 400 to finish the season in fourth place.

It was a strong finish to a season in which Kenseth continued to prove that he is one of racing's top drivers.

CAREER STATISTICS

Year	Rank	Starts	Wins	Poles
2007	4	36	2	0
2006	2	36	4	0
2005	7	36	1	2
2004	8	36	2	0
2003	1	36	1	0
2002	8	36	5	1
2001	13	36	0	0
2000	14	34	1	0
1999	49	5	0	0
1998	57	1	0	0

Top 5	Top 10	Earnings	Points
13	22	$6,485,630	6,298
15	21	$6,608,920	6,419
12	17	$5,790,770	6,352
8	16	$6,223,890	6,069
11	25	$4,038,120	5,022
11	19	$3,888,850	4,432
4	9	$2,265,840	3,982
4	11	$2,150,760	3,711
1	1	$143,561	434
0	1	$42,340	150

CAREER ACHIEVEMENTS

- **Winston Cup champion in 2003.**

- **Earned Winston Cup Raybestos Rookie of the Year honors in 2000.**

- **Racked up a career-best fifteen top-five finishes in 2006.**

- **Finished the 2006 season with a career best 9.8 average finish and a career best 14.6 average start.**

- **Led a career high 1,132 laps during the 2006 Nextel Cup season.**

- **Finished second in the Nextel Cup standings in 2006, his highest finish since claiming the Cup title in 2003.**

- **Has finished no lower than eighth in the Cup standings since 2002.**

- Won his first Cup race, the Coca-Cola 600 at Lowe's Motor Speedway, in 2000 in only his eighteenth career start.

- Made his Winston Cup debut at Dover Downs in 1998 and finished sixth.

- Finished second in the Busch series standings in 1998 and third in 1999.

- Finished second in the Busch series rookie battle in 1997 despite making only twenty-one starts.

- Finished third in the Hooters series in 1996.

CHAPTER NOTES

CHAPTER 1. ROOKIE OF THE YEAR

1. Shav Glick, "Kenseth takes the inside track," *Milwaukee Journal Sentinel*, July 2, 2000, <http://findarticles.com/p/articles/mi_qn4196/is_20000702/ai_n10627969> (November 4, 2006).

2. "Matt Kenseth Coca-Cola Recap," *Roushracing.com*, May 28, 2000, <http://www.roushracing.com.matt_kenseth/archive.asp?yr=2000> (November 3, 2006).

3. "Matt Kenseth Captures 2000 Raybestos Rookie of the Year Title," *Mattkenseth.com*, <http://www.mattkenseth.com/news/2000/news2000-1112.html> (November 3, 2006).

4. "Matt Kenseth Daytona 500 Recap," *Roushracing.com*, February 20, 2000, <http://www.roushracing.com.matt_kenseth/archive.asp?yr=2000> (November 3, 2006).

5. "Rain shortened race at Las Vegas," *Mattkenseth.com*, March 15, 2000, <http://www.mattkenseth.com/news/2000/news2000-03.html> (November 3, 2006).

6. "Matt Kenseth Mall.com 400 Recap," *Roushracing.com*, March 19, 2000, <http://www.roushracing.com.matt_kenseth/archive.asp?yr=2000> (November 3, 2006).

CHAPTER 2. GROWING UP IN WISCONSIN

1. Larry Woody, "NASCAR's unknown soldier: Matt Kenseth won more races than any other Winston cup driver last season – so why didn't anyone notice?" *Auto Racing Digest*, August-September, 2003, <http://findarticles.com/p/articles/mi_m0FCH/is_5_31/ai_103563730> (November 10, 2006).

2. Mark McCarter, "Hiding in plain sight," *Sporting News*, April 28, 2003, <http://www.findarticles.com/p/articles/mi_m1208/is_17_227/ai_100728370> (November 10, 2006).

3. Larry Woody, "NASCAR's unknown soldier: Matt Kenseth won more races than any other Winston cup driver last season – so why didn't anyone notice?" *Auto Racing Digest*, August-September, 2003, <http://findarticles.com/p/articles/mi_m0FCH/is_5_31/ai_103563730> (November 10, 2006).

4. Mike Hembree, "The Mystery Man," *SceneDaily.com*, May 19, 2003, <http://www.scenedaily.com/stories/2003/05/19/scene_story2.html> (November 6, 2006).

5. Dave Kallman, "Racing runs in the blood," *Milwaukee Journal Sentinel*, February 8, 2000, <http://www.findarticles.com/p/articles/mi_qn4196/is_20000208/ai_n10579042> (November 7, 2006).

6. Ibid.

7. Shav Glick, "Kenseth takes the inside track," *Milwaukee Journal Sentinel*, July 2, 2000, <http://findarticles.com/p/articles/mi_qn4196/is_20000702/ai_n10627969> (November 4, 2006).

8. Melanie Fonder, "Hometown Hero: Matt Kenseth puts Cambridge on the map," *No Limits*, 2004, <http://www.nolimitswisconsin.com/Study/HometownHero.html> (November 7, 2006).

9. Mark McCarter, "Hiding in plain sight," *Sporting News*, April 28, 2003, <http://www.findarticles.com/p/articles/mi_m1208/is_17_227/ai_100728370> (November 10, 2006).

CHAPTER 3. GETTING DOWN AND DIRTY

1. Dave Kallman, "Racing runs in the blood," *Milwaukee Journal Sentinel*, February 8, 2000, <http://www.findarticles.com/p/articles/mi_qn4196/is_20000208/ai_n10579042> (November 7, 2006).

2. Ibid.

3. Dave Kallman, "Kenseth driving toward the 'majors'" *Milwaukee Journal Sentinel*, July 11, 1995, <http://findarticles.com/p/articles/mi_qn4196/is_19950711/ai_10200768> (November 9, 2006).

4. Sheridan A. Glen, "Runnin' with the big dogs," July 2002, <http://www.madisonmagazine.com/article.php?section_id=918&xstate=view_story&story_id=113811> (November 8, 2006).

5. "Weekly Battles at Slinger Helped Prepare Kenseth for Winston Cup," *RoushRacing.com*, April 11, 2000, <http://www.roushracing.com/matt_kenseth/archive.asp?yr=2000> (November 3, 2006).

6. Ibid.

CHAPTER 4. SUCCESS IN THE BUSCH SERIES

1. Dave Kallman, "Auto Racing," *Milwaukee Journal Sentinel*, April 16, 1997, <http://findarticles.com/p/articles/mi_qn4196/is_19970416/ai_n10326355> (November 9, 2006).

2. Mike Hembree, "The Mystery Man," *SceneDaily.com*, May 19, 2003, <http://www.scenedaily.com/stories/2003/05/19/scene_story2.html> (November 6, 2006).

3. Mark McCarter, "Hiding in plain sight," *Sporting News*, April 28, 2003, <http://www.findarticles.com/p/articles/mi_m1208/is_17_227/ai_100728370> (November 10, 2006).

4. Dave Kallman, "Kenseth to stay with Reiser team," *Milwaukee Journal Sentinel*, April 28, 1997, <http://findarticles.com/p/articles/mi_qn4196/is_19970428/ai_n10341800> (November 9, 2006).

5. Ibid.

6. Mike Hembree, "The Mystery Man," *SceneDaily.com*, May 19, 2003, <http://www.scenedaily.com/stories/2003/05/19/scene_story2.html> (November 6, 2006).

CHAPTER 5. MENTORS SHAPE KENSETH'S FUTURE

1. Scoop Malinowski, "The Biofiles: Matt Kenseth," *CBS.Sportsline.com*, June 6, 2006, <http://cbs.sportsline.com/spin/story/9482404> (November 4, 2006).

2. Jesse Osborne, "Kenseth excited about return to MIS," *Wisconsin State Journal*, May 7, 2003, <http://www.madison.com/wisconsinstatejournal/sports48418.php> (November 7, 2006).

3. Ibid.

4. Dave Kallman, "Racing runs in the blood," *Milwaukee Journal Sentinel*, February 8, 2000, <http://www.findarticles.com/p/articles/mi_qn4196/is_20000208/ai_n10579042> (November 7, 2006).

5. Stephen Sferazo, "Getting to know Matt Kenseth," *SpeedwayMedia.com*, July 25, 2006, <http://www.speedwaymedia.com/Articles/06/072506Sferazo.asp> (November 7, 2006).

6. Larry Woody, "NASCAR's unknown soldier," *Auto Racing Digest*, August-September, 2003, <http://www.findarticles.com/p/articles/mi_m0FCH/is_5_31/ai_103563730> (November 10, 2006).

7. "Mark's protégé: Up-and-comer Matt Kenseth," *MarkMartin.org*, 1999, <http://www.markmartin.org/kenseth.html> (November 11, 2006).

8. Larry Woody, "NASCAR's unknown soldier," *Auto Racing Digest*, August-September, 2003, <http://www.findarticles.com/p/articles/mi_m0FCH/is_5_31/ai_103563730> (November 10, 2006).

9. Barry Wilner, "The Fastest Learner – race drive Matt Kenseth," *Auto Racing Digest*, October, 2001, <http://www.findarticles.com/p/articles/mi_m0FCH/is_6_29/ai_77702404> (November 10, 2006).

10. Ibid.

11. "Mark's protégé: Up-and-comer Matt Kenseth," *MarkMartin.org*, 1999, <http://www.markmartin.org/kenseth.html> (November 11, 2006).

12. Ibid.

13. Ibid.

CHAPTER 6. A FUTURE STAR IS BORN

1. Dave Kallmann, "A near-triumphant return," *Milwaukee Journal Sentinel*, November 9, 2003, <http://findarticles.com/p/articles/mi_qn4196/is_20031109/ai_n10929011> (November 11, 2006).

2. Ibid.

3. "Chat Transcript: Matt Kenseth," *NASCAR.com*, March 20, 2002, <http://www.nascar.com/2002/comm/chat/03/20/kenseth_transcript/index.html> (November 9, 2006).

4. Dave Kallmann, "Kenseth's sparkling run wins over stock-car fans," *Milwaukee Journal Sentinel*, September 25, 1998, <http://findarticles.com/p/articles/mi_qn4196/is_19980925/ai_n10455200> (November 7, 2006).

5. Ibid.

6. Ibid

7. Mike Hembree, "The Mystery Man," *SceneDaily.com*, May 19, 2003, <http://www.scenedaily.com/stories/2003/05/19/scene_story2.html> (November 6, 2006).

CHAPTER 7. THE SOPHOMORE SLUMP

1. "Matt Kenseth: Rookie No More," *MattKenseth.com*, February 5, 2001, <http://www.mattkenseth.com/news/2001/news2001-0102.html> (November 7, 2006).

2. Ibid.

3. "DuraLube 400, North Carolina Motor Speedway," *MattKenseth.com*, February 27, 2001, <http://www.mattkenseth.com/news/2001/news2001-0102.html> (November 7, 2006).

4. Mark McCarter, "Hiding in plain sight," *Sporting News*, April 28, 2003, <http://www.findarticles.com/p/articles/mi_m1208/is_17_227/ai_100728370> (November 10, 2006).

5. Larry Cothren, "Stock Car Racing Feature Stories: Matt Kenseth," *Stockcarracing.com*, 2002, <http://www.stockcarracing.com/thehistoryof/93758_matt_kenseth_interview/index.html> (November 8, 2006).

6. Ibid.

7. Dave Kallman, "Kenseth leaves all his troubles behind," *Milwaukee Journal Sentinel*, April 3, 2002, <http://www.findarticles.com/p/articles/mi_qn4196/is_20020403/ai_n10782410> (November 7, 2006).

8. Larry Cothren, "Stock Car Racing Feature Stories: Matt Kenseth," *Stockcarracing.com*, 2002, <http://www.stockcarracing.com/thehistoryof/93758_matt_kenseth_interview/index.html> (November 8, 2006).

9. Lee Montgomery, "Kenseth Catches Yellow," *RacingOne. com*, February 24, 2002, <http://www.racingone.com/article/aspx?artnum=12434> (November 13, 2006).

10. Mark McCarter, "Hiding in plain sight," *Sporting News*, April 28, 2003, <http://www.findarticles.com/p/articles/mi_m1208/is_17_227/ai_100728370> (November 10, 2006).

CHAPTER 8. BECOMING A CHAMPION

1. "Daytona 500 Race Recap," *MattKenseth.com*, February 17, 2003, <http://nascar.about.com/gi/dynamic/offsite.htm?site=http://www.mattkenseth.com> (November 12, 2006).

2. "UAW-DaimlerChrysler 400 Race Recap," *MattKenseth.com*, March 3, 2003, <http://nascar.about.com/gi/dynamic/offsite.htm?site=http://www.mattkenseth.com> (November 12, 2006).

3. Mike Hembree, "The Mystery Man," *SceneDaily.com*, May 19, 2003, <http://www.scenedaily.com/stories/2003/05/19/scene_story2.html> (November 6, 2006).

4. Rupen Fofaria, "Kenseth prefers life out of the limelight," *ESPN.com*, July 23, 2003, <http://espn.go.com/rpm/wc/2003/0723/1584680.html> (November 16, 2006).

5. Ibid.

6. "Matt Kenseth Claims NASCAR Winston Cup Championship," *Motortrend.com*, November 10, 2003, <http://www.motortrend.com/features/auto_news/112_news_031111_nascar/> (November 12, 2006).

7. Bill Center, "NASCAR chasing...after Kenseth," *San Diego Union-Tribune*, September 1, 2006, <http://www.signonsandiego.com/uniontrib/20060901/news_1s1nextel.html> (November 8, 2006).

8. Marty Smith, "Conversation: Matt Kenseth," *Turner Sports Interactive*, December 3, 2003, <http://www.nascar.com/2003/news/features/conversation/12/03/mkenseth_conversation/index.html> (November 7, 2006).

CHAPTER 9. MATT KENSETH, THE COMMON MAN

1. Paul Newberry, "Kenseth old-fashioned – and proud of it," *Chicago Sun-Times*, February 12, 2004, <http://www.findarticles.com/p/articles/mi_qn4155/is_20040212/ai_n12531628> (November 16, 2006).

2. Holly Cain, "Kenseth keeps low profile everywhere but on track," *Seattle Post-Intelligencer*, November 15, 2003, <http://www.seattlepi.nwsource.com/motorsports/148444_auto15.html> (November 16, 2006).

3. Paul Newberry, "Kenseth old-fashioned – and proud of it," *Chicago Sun-Times*, February 12, 2004, <http://www.findarticles.com/p/articles/mi_qn4155/is_20040212/ai_n12531628> (November 16, 2006).

4. Larry Cothren, "Stock Car Racing Feature Stories: Matt Kenseth," *Stockcarracing.com*, 2002, <http://www.stockcarracing.com/thehistoryof/93758_matt_kenseth_interview/index.html> (November 8, 2006).

5. Ibid.

6. Holly Cain, "Kenseth keeps low profile everywhere but on track," *Seattle Post-Intelligencer*, November 15, 2003, <http://www.seattlepi.nwsource.com/motorsports/148444_auto15.html> (November 16, 2006).

7. Tom Alesia, "Kenseth a real winner with his fans," *Wisconsin State Journal*, 2002, <http://www.madison.com/wisconsinstatejournal/sports/8895.html> (November 12, 2006).

8. Lee Spencer, "Powerful rivals, but better friends," *Sporting News*, May 5, 2004, <http://www.msnbc.msn.com/id/4894282> (November 7, 2006).

9. Mike Hembree, "The Mystery Man," *SceneDaily.com*, May 19, 2003, <http://www.scenedaily.com/stories/2003/05/19/scene_story2.html> (November 6, 2006).

10. Jenna Fryer, "Matt Kenseth Journal: Top 10 at New Hampshire a surprise," *Sportsline.com*, 2006, <http://www.sportsline.com/autoracing/story/9671525> (November 13, 2006).

11. Ibid.

12. Sarah Rothschild, "Off the track with Matt Kenseth," *MiamiHerald. com*, September 29, 2006, <http://www.miami.com/mld/miamiherald/ sports/motorsports/15635423.htm?source=rss&channel=miamiherald_ motorsports> (November 16, 2006).

13. Dave Kallmann, "Kenseth's plane fancy; Driver following granddad's passion," *Milwaukee Journal Sentinel*, March 12, 2006, <http://www.findarticles.com/p/articles/mi_qn4196/is_20060312/ai_ n16155560> (November 13, 2006).

CHAPTER 10: SEEKING THE ELUSIVE SECOND TITLE

1. "Kenseth hits Vegas Jackpot," *Roushracing.com*, March 7, 2004, <http://www.roushracing.com/matt_kenseth/articles/dh030704_153. htm> (November 19, 2006).

2. Ibid.

3. "Dover hopes dashed," *Roushracing.com*, September 26, 2004, <http://www.roushracing.com/matt_kenseth/articles/dh092604_180. htm> (November 19, 2006).

4. "We'll be back," *Roushracing.com*, December 3, 2004, <http:// www.roushracing.com/matt_kenseth/articles/db122004_200.htm> (November 19, 2006).

5. "Matt Kenseth finishes second in Richmond – Secures Spot in Chase for Championship," *Roushracing.com*, September 12, 2005, <http://www. roushracing.com/matt_kenseth/articles/dh091205_215.htm> (November 19, 2006).

6. "Tire Problems Result in 35th Place Finish for Matt Kenseth – Falls to 9th in Championship Standings," *Roushracing.com*, September 26, 2005, <http://www.roushracing.com/matt_kenseth/articles/dh092605_ 217.htm> (November 19, 2006).

7. "Kenseth Encounters Brake Problem in Phoenix – Finishes 32nd," *Roushracing.com*, November 14, 2005, <http://www.roushracing.com/ matt_kenseth/articles/dh111405_224.htm> (November 19, 2006).

8. Bill Center, "NASCAR chasing...after Kenseth," *San Diego Union-Tribune*, September 1, 2006, <http://www.signonsandiego.com/ uniontrib/20060901/news_1s1nextel.html> (November 8, 2006).

9. "Kenseth Enters Chase as Series' Points Leader; Finishes Eighth at Richmond," *Roushracing.com*, September 9, 2006, <http://www. roushracing.com/matt_kenseth/articles/dh090906_254.htm> (November 19, 2006).

10. "Matt Kenseth and Carl Edwards talk the rest of the '06 season and on to '07," *Backstretchmotorsports.com*, October 18, 2006, <http://www.backstretchmotorsports.com/bm/index.php?option=com_content&task-view&id=8227&itemid=29> (November 18, 2006).

11. "Party crasher," *SportsIllustrated.com*, October 29, 2006, <http://www.sportsillustrated.cnn.com/2006/racing/10/29/nascar.atlanta.ap/index.html> (November 18, 2006).

12. Dave Kallmann, "Kenseth's course hits a bump; Racer can't explain," *Milwaukee Journal Sentinel*, November 12, 2006, <http://www.findarticles.com/p/articles/mi_qn4169/is_20061112/ai_n16841536> (November 20, 2006).

13. Dave Kallmann, "The silver lining," *Milwaukee Journal Sentinel,* December 1, 2006, <http://www.findarticles.com/p/articles/mi_qn4169/is_20061201/ai_n16908734> (December 5, 2006).

14. Beau Estes, "Kenseth continues to dominate sport – quietly," *nascar.com*, September 11, 2007, <http://www.nascar.com/2007/news/opinion/09/04/bestes.mkenseth.convo/index.html> (November 15, 2007).

GLOSSARY

banking—The sloping of a racetrack, particularly at a curve or a corner.

chassis—The combination of a car's floorboard, interior, and roll cage.

draft—The aerodynamic effect that allows two or more cars traveling nose-to-tail to run faster than a single car. When one car follows closely, the one in front cuts through the air, providing less resistance for the car in back.

pit road—The area where pit crews service the cars.

pole—Slang term for the first position on the starting grid, awarded to the fastest qualifier.

setup—Slang term for the tuning and adjustments made to a racecar's suspension before and during a race.

short track—Racetracks that are less than one mile (1.6 km) in length.

Superspeedway—A racetrack of one mile (1.6 km) or more in distance.

tight—A car is said to be tight if the front wheels lose traction before the rear wheels do.

Victory Lane—Sometimes called the "winner's circle." The spot on each racetrack's infield where the race winner parks for the celebration.

FOR MORE INFORMATION

WEB LINKS

The official Matt Kenseth fan site:
www.mattkenseth.com

The official site of NASCAR:
www.NASCAR.com

The site of ESPN:
www.ESPN.com

The site of Fox Sports:
www.foxsports.com

FURTHER READING

Maruszewski, Kelley. *Matt Kenseth: Above and Beyond*. Champaign, IL: Sports Publishing L.L.C., 2004.

Maruszewski, Kelley. *Matt Kenseth: Midwest Sensation (Racing Superstar Series)*. Champaign, IL: Sports Publishing L.L.C., 2003.

INDEX